Praise for *The Silk Road Rediscovered*

"To become really global, Indian business must extend its footprint to China. *The Silk Road Rediscovered* is a must-read for those who wish to understand the challenges of doing so and assess the opportunities that it offers. Based on detailed case studies, this book is really the only practitioner's guide on this subject. Equally, it offers valuable insights into the mirror image story still unfolding—the arrival of brand China in India. That is already making an impact in many ways. What Gupta, Pande, and Wang offer is a look at an economic future to which the rest of us have not yet fully woken up."

—**S. Jaishankar**, Ambassador of India to the United States and former Ambassador to China

"By 2050, China and India will probably have the two largest economies in the world. Success is not guaranteed. Yet it is also clear that if they cooperate, they will rise together. This book could not be timelier. Gupta, Pande, and Wang explain well how companies in both countries can leverage off each other. If they do this, they will also help to preserve peace between Asia's two giants."

—**Kishore Mahbubani**, dean, Lee Kuan Yew School of Public Policy, National University of Singapore and author of *The Great Convergence*

"As two potential global giants, the Dragon and the Tiger will inevitably have to learn to live together, work together, and aspire to a convergence of interests. One of the best ways to do this is through business. This book is a timely reminder of the need to rediscover, indeed to reinvent, the Silk Road that once bound these two nations together. This is easier said than done. There are, as of now, wide differences in terms of political ideologies, geopolitical realities, and cultural mindsets. However, these are all part of the excitement of doing business in a globalized world. *The Silk Road Rediscovered* encapsulates the steep learning curve experienced by Indian companies doing business in China and by pioneering Chinese companies that have chosen to put their faith and money in India. It distills the lessons learned to produce a strategic roadmap. With its trenchant analysis and wide as well as deep perspective, this book is an indispensable guide for anyone planning to travel the new Silk Road."

—**Anand Mahindra**, chairman and managing director, Mahindra & Mahindra

"Without any doubt, market size and the quality of talent available in any country are highly relevant factors for almost every company. This central fact makes the Chinese and Indian markets extremely important for companies based in these countries. *The Silk Road Rediscovered* provides a brilliant analysis of how Chinese and Indian companies are strengthening their competitive advantage by leveraging the unique strengths of each country, integrating these strengths globally, and ensuring management consistency during the globalization process. I recommend this book highly to the leaders of not only Chinese and Indian companies but also to those of any aspiring global enterprise."

> —**Guo Ping**, deputy chairman and rotating CEO, Huawei Technologies

"China and India are rapidly on the way to becoming two of the most important planks of the global economy. Unfortunately, mutual suspicion has held back stronger cooperation between these two countries. Anyone who has worked in these two countries can recognize the tremendous growth that can occur if companies in India and China better understand each other. Based on analyses of pioneering companies from both sides, *The Silk Road Rediscovered* provides a timely strategic roadmap for Chinese and Indian companies to succeed in each other's markets. A strong by-product will be an improvement in relations between the two countries. I view this book as essential reading for not only corporate executives but also policy makers interested in the China-India relationship."

> —**Ajit Rangnekar**, dean, Indian School of Business

"*The Silk Road Rediscovered* directs the searchlight on a key global relationship, between India and China, focusing on their economic ties. The authors pithily say that this is just 'Day One' in the evolution of this relationship. There are tremendous opportunities and also redoubtable challenges ahead. Instant gratification is not guaranteed but long-term commitments are vital. For Chinese companies particularly, there is need for rapid learning and understanding the rich diversity of India. It is this focus on the big picture that captures attention as the authors take us through the experience, the dos and don'ts of doing business in either country. The takeaway is that the two countries must take advantage of the cascade of opportunities that lie ahead, learning from the past few years, and forging through this process, a resilient and strong relationship that buttresses economic development for mutual benefit. An important study, deserving a thumbs-up from all students of the India-China relationship."

> —**Nirupama Rao**, former Foreign Secretary, Ministry of External Affairs, India and former Ambassador of India to China and the United States

"As China and India grow to become even bigger economic giants, trade and investment linkages between them will grow exponentially. It is imperative that companies from India as well as China figure out how to engage with the other country in order to not only win locally but also become stronger globally. As we know from the experience of Tata companies, doing so requires conviction, creativity, and commitment. *The Silk Road Rediscovered* is a pioneering book written by authors Gupta, Pande, and Wang who are well-versed with increasing commercial ties between both countries. The book lays out the case for mutual engagement and provides detailed analyses of the evolutionary journeys of Indian companies in China and Chinese companies in India."

—**Ratan N. Tata**, chairman, Tata Group (1991–2012)

"The spectacular growth of China over the past thirty years and that of India in the past fifteen years are unprecedented in the annals of human history and are the inspiration for the rest of the emerging economies worldwide. Never before have we had so many people lift themselves from poverty and realize their dreams in such a short time in recorded history. Until recently, however, these two great economies had been growing despite each other and often in rivalry for the world's attention and its investments. That has changed and Chinese and Indian companies are discovering their respective markets and creating greater economic benefit for all with far greater implications for their own worldwide market success. That story has been largely untold until now. *The Silk Road Rediscovered* is a pioneering work that should be on the desk of every global manager and every MBA student with its chapter headings akin to the headlines that are shaping the modern day world. Gupta, Pande, and Wang have left a legacy that will inspire many keen observers of global forces shaping our world."

—**Shane Tedjarati**, president and CEO, Honeywell Global High Growth Regions

The Silk Road Rediscovered

HOW INDIAN AND CHINESE
COMPANIES ARE BECOMING
GLOBALLY STRONGER BY WINNING
IN EACH OTHER'S MARKETS

Anil K. Gupta

Girija Pande

Haiyan Wang

JB JOSSEY-BASS™

A Wiley Brand

Cover design by Adrian Morgan
Cover image: © Thinkstock and Shutterstock

Copyright © 2014 by John Wiley and Sons. All rights reserved.

Published by Jossey-Bass
A Wiley Brand
One Montgomery Street, Suite 1200, San Francisco, CA 94104-4594—
www.josseybass.com

Jossey-Bass books and products are available through most bookstores. To contact Jossey-Bass directly call our Customer Care Department within the U.S. at 800-956-7739, outside the U.S. at 317-572-3986, or fax 317-572-4002.

Wiley publishes in a variety of print and electronic formats and by print-on-demand. Some material included with standard print versions of this book may not be included in e-books or in print-on-demand. If this book refers to media such as a CD or DVD that is not included in the version you purchased, you may download this material at **http://booksupport.wiley.com**. For more information about Wiley products, visit **www.wiley.com**.

The Library of Congress Cataloging-in-Publication data is on file.

ISBN 978-1-1184-4623-2 (cloth),
ISBN 978-1-1188-9601-3 (pdf),
ISBN 978-1-1188-9593-1 (epub)

Printed in the United States of America
FIRST EDITION
HB Printing   10 9 8 7 6 5 4 3 2 1

Contents

Foreword

Are India and China natural rivals? Do their deeply different and contrasting histories, cultures, institutions, and economies lead them to compete in a zero-sum manner? Or can these near reverse-image giants complement and attract one another, building a common future? The fate of one-third of humanity lies in the balance of these questions.

For nearly a half century, the dominant view of American political and economic leaders has been that Asia's two great civilizations are destined to clash. Asia's two giants have given little reason for foreigners to believe that they are capable of forging a common future.

I have experienced the pessimistic view first hand—in America, and in both India and China. My first glimpse was in Washington, DC. In November 2011, before departing for my own five-month study tour across Asia, I met with a senior U.S. government official responsible for policy toward China. In the center of his coffee table was one book, and only one book. It was Robert Kaplan's latest: *Monsoon: The Indian Ocean and the Future of American Power*. Kaplan's compelling travelogue explored strategic investments by Chinese state-owned companies in ports surrounding India and also examined India's emerging strengths as a democracy and market economy.

Many senior U.S. officials bought Kaplan's argument, sharing his view that the U.S. should take advantage of the tension between Chinese state-driven capitalism and India's emerging high-tech democracy. For the United States, stronger ties with India could serve as a counterweight to China. This asymmetric treatment of the world's two largest nations would become a centerpiece of the Obama administration's "pivot to Asia."

Seeing Indian and Chinese differences as the basis for a rivalry to be exploited is a time-tested tradition in U.S. foreign policy. Senior officials in the Truman, Eisenhower, and Kennedy administrations all saw democratic India as a bulwark against communist China. President Nixon's détente with China turned those tables around. America soon became fascinated with a more open and capitalistic China, and began to compare it to a sclerotic India, mired in an archaic caste system and endemic corruption. It took another two decades for the pendulum to swing back toward India, only after the Tiananmen Square event and China's growing export prowess began to steer American leaders toward a more wary assessment. Presidents Clinton and Bush began to explore a deeper relationship with a more liberal and resurgent India as a like-minded ally.

Regardless of which way these American officials leaned, they were all inclined to focus on the differences between China and India. And who can blame them? Anyone who has spent time in India and China immediately focuses on the contrasts, and tries to assess them. Many have sided with the enormous economic success of China. When travelling with my family in 2012, my eight-year-old daughter seemed to take this perspective. As we arrived in Beijing after nine weeks in India, and sped down a modern freeway toward our steel-and-glass service apartment, she said approvingly, "Daddy, this looks more like America." The Chinese emphasis on manufacturing, infrastructure, and social order make China's leading cities appear to be modern, Asian versions of Western cities.

By contrast, Indian cities appear more chaotic, interspersing glimpses of modernity with cows wandering aimlessly through city traffic. Slums jostle right alongside downtown business districts. Driving down an Indian road is multitasking for the senses—with a panorama of colors, a cacophony of horns and bells, smells of sewage and incense, and the grit and dust of roads in transition.

Still, for all of India's chaos, there is much for an American to admire, if not love. The country's deep commitment to democracy, freedom of speech and press, protection of religious minorities, and attention to the rural poor remain its long-term strength. China's far more hierarchical, authoritarian culture, with little public debate, seems opaque to most Americans. When that system seemed to work, many foreigners were willing to dismiss its moral failings. But in recent years, its ineffectiveness has begun to shine through. China's economic growth has slowed and it also has left in its wake staggering air pollution, toxic rivers, unsafe food, and rampant corruption.

But do these stark differences automatically lead to rivalry for the world's two most populous countries? Or are they an opportunity for greater cooperation? At its most basic level, international trade and investment have been all about making matches when two nations have complementary assets.

That is the starting point for Anil Gupta, Girija Pande, and Haiyan Wang's terrific volume. In seeing Chinese and Indian differences as an opportunity, they have been careful to stay away from misty-eyed optimism. A major strength of this book is that Gupta, Pande, and Wang start with what works. Whether it is Indian tech instructors helping Chinese universities or Chinese manufacturers working on the ground in India, the specific details show that cooperation is real—and really valuable.

These successes, in turn, speak to broader common themes emerging in both countries. Throughout this volume, the authors remind the reader of deeper trends and histories in both countries that potentially bind them together. Several of those themes are worth noting upfront.

First and foremost, each in their own way, both countries have made a basic commitment to private enterprise. That commitment is not to be taken lightly. Resistance to capitalism lingers in these two nations that still, on paper, call themselves communist and socialist. Still, it is the growing role of the private sector that is expanding cooperation between both countries.

Gupta, Pande, and Wang's work is so critical because, for that commitment to succeed, these nations need to reinforce in one another the centrality of market forces to economic growth. Much in the same way that France and Germany learned to make their market economies complement one another as the anchor for a Europe whole and free, China and India will need to match their market economies if growth is going to bind Asia.

Similarly, both countries are committed to technological modernization—even if they often are getting there via very different paths. That joint commitment means that both countries value science and technology as a driver of commerce. As any businessperson knows, successfully commercializing a scientific breakthrough involves taking the insights of any particular technologist and building repetitive processes that are then sold at scale to a wide range of consumers. That requires a trained workforce—whether in refining that technology or simply using advanced manufacturing inputs. India and China each have national strengths in that life-arch. India brings terrific technology schools, an aspiration of its top companies toward world-class intellectual property protection, and a history of large corporate investments. China's enormous strengths are almost perfectly complementary: logistics, mass manufacturing, strategic focus, and marketing.

The word *convergence* appears regularly in this volume. In technical terms, that marks China's shift away from investment and manufacturing and toward services and consumption.

And for India, that means the exact opposite. But more broadly, the real convergence that seems to underline this trend is one about values. For China, the switch to a consumption-oriented, service economy has meant allowing its people to enjoy the fruits of their labor and to be more open in expressing a range of views and opinions. For instance, my entire family noted with fascination the enormous interest in

Buddhism—and with religion in general—among the rising generation of Chinese. In India, the attention to manufacturing and infrastructure means harnessing a swirling, spiritually heterogeneous society, and bringing a greater discipline in the pursuit of material success. While attachment to religious identities remains strong in India, the new focus on materialism has certainly begun to erode some ancient institutions, such as the caste system.

That convergence is taking place as both countries struggle with major social upheaval. In both countries, a small handful of cities and provinces/states has produced the lion's share of wealth in the last three decades. Hundreds of millions of poor have flocked toward major cities in search of work. As both countries have tried to create jobs—both for migrants and for those left behind in their hinterlands—taking advantage of local resources has been critical. These enormous social forces are taking place across vast human populations—where in both China and India, a medium-sized province or state is often as large as a major European country.

One of the great lessons of *The Silk Road Rediscovered* is how much these local characteristics come into play in the strategic decisions and actions of companies, in both directions. Gupta, Pande, and Wang provide a business-oriented look at unique local flavors when it comes to doing business in each place. They dispel the notion that a single approach will work in the world's two most populous countries. The emerging company-to-company, city-to-city, and state-to-province connections are crisscrossing the Himalayas, connecting Shenzhen's Huawei to an R&D center in Bangalore, Mumbai's Tata Motors to a manufacturing facility in Chongqing, and Gurgaon's NIIT to its university partners in Shanghai, Wuxi, Chongqing, and Chengdu. In fact, the level of detail in this book reinforces the extraordinary diversity within both countries. Their parallel diversities, convergences, and growing economic links might just as well be called *New Silk Roads Discovered*.

Yet amidst all this local diversity, the authors are quite attuned to the global context in which this cooperation takes place. They constantly remind strategists not only to think long-term, but also to think in global terms. Each different local player in China and India fits into wider regional and global trading and investment networks. Trade and investment between these two giants will not work simply because one part of India invests in one part of China, or vice versa. Successful strategies will place that bilateral cooperation into the global system of trade and investment. It is that kind of far-sighted global vision that will lead to success in the twenty-first century.

William Antholis, Washington, DC, January 2014

William Antholis is managing director of the Brookings Institution and a senior fellow in Governance Studies. He has served in the U.S. government at the White House and the State Department. He is the author of *Inside Out, India and China: Local Politics Go Global* and coauthor with Strobe Talbott of *Fast Forward: Ethics and Politics in the Age of Global Warming*.

Preface

In May 2013, barely two months after his election by the Communist Party Congress, Premier Li Keqiang embarked on his maiden official visit outside China. The first stop on his tour? A three-day visit to India—a clear signal of China's foreign policy priorities. Upon his arrival, the premier remarked, "We are one-third of the world's total population and our interactions attract the world. Without doubt, China-India relations are [among the] most important global relations."

Like many neighbors, the relationship between India and China remains full of tensions, economic as well as geopolitical, and they are unlikely to melt anytime soon. We predict, however, that by 2025, economic ties between the two countries will be among the ten most important bilateral ties in the world. It is a near certainty that by then, China and India will rank among the four largest economies in the world. Both are also launching global champions across a range of industries from technology (Tata Consultancy Services [TCS], Infosys, Huawei, and Lenovo) to heavy manufacturing (Tata Motors, Mahindra,

Geely, and Chery) to consumer goods (Godrej and Shuanghui). Given the size and growth rate of the two economies, Chinese and Indian companies with global ambitions have little choice but to look across the Himalayas and see one of the world's largest markets sitting right next door.

Economic ties between India and China have been dominated so far by trade rather than investment. Bilateral trade between the two grew from less than US$3 billion in 2000 to US$69 billion in 2012—an annual growth rate of almost 30 percent, significantly faster than the 19.4-percent and 19.2-percent annual growth rates, respectively, in China's and India's trades with the rest of the world, or the 9.2-percent growth rate in world trade. In contrast, the stock of direct investment has been small. However, the picture is changing rapidly. India's Mahindra Group is now the fifth-largest tractor manufacturer in China with a market share of about 9–10 percent. Tata Motors' Jaguar Land Rover subsidiary (JLR) has been the fastest growing luxury auto seller in China over the last five years and is now investing in a manufacturing plant as well as R&D facilities. China's Huawei has had its second largest R&D center in Bangalore since the late 1990s and currently employs about five thousand people in India. Lenovo is one of the top three PC companies in India. And Haier, the home appliance giant, currently manufactures refrigerators at a plant in Pune. These are just some of the new developments presently under way and illustrate how some of the pioneering Indian and Chinese companies are busy rediscovering the fabled Silk Road that in ancient times joined their nations and served as the avenue for economic links and mutual learning.

This is the first book ever to analyze the growing corporate linkages between India and China. The book's uniqueness also derives from the fact that it combines the authors' academic rigor with their wide-ranging and deep executive and consulting experience. Importantly, it also brings together the authors' diverse national backgrounds as well as upbringing and professional experience across several cornerstone economies—India, China, Singapore, and the United States. We trace the historical ties between the two civilizations, the recent history of geopolitical tensions between them, how their citizens view each other, and the future of economic links between them. We look at the potential opportunities and challenges that China will offer during the coming decade to foreign companies, including those from India. We present insightful case studies of the China journeys of several well-known Indian companies including TCS, Mahindra Tractors, NIIT, and Tata Motors/Jaguar Land Rover. These case studies may inspire and offer lessons to other Indian companies contemplating a move into China. The book also includes several case studies of pioneering Chinese companies—Lenovo, Huawei, TBEA, Haier, and Xinxing Heavy Machinery—that have made a strong commitment to India and are beginning to realize the fruits of this commitment. We close by offering a China-focused strategic roadmap for Indian companies.

The book is targeted at the leaders of Indian and Chinese multinationals for whom the other country could be a supplier, a customer, a competitor, and a partner, and who view their Himalayan neighbor with a sense of mystery and perhaps trepidation. It should also be of high value to the leaders of multinational corporations (MNCs) in the United States, Europe, Japan, South Korea, and other countries. The success of major Indian and Chinese companies in each other's markets is bound to strengthen them, whet their appetite for further global expansion, and create greater competition in the future. Growing economic integration between India and China will also offer new opportunities as well as new competitive challenges to all multinationals. Thus it is important for MNC executives to know what is transpiring. Finally, we anticipate that the book will also be of great interest to policy makers and scholars as well as business students worldwide with an interest in the rise of global champions from China and India.

Chapter One discusses the evolving ties between India and China. While the primary focus of this chapter is on economic linkages, we begin with a discussion of the historical ties between the two civilizations, the recent history of geopolitical tensions between them, and how their citizens view each other. This multifaceted examination of cross-country ties is important because economic relations are embedded in cultural linkages, personal attitudes, and geopolitical relationships. The chapter goes on to look at the factors constraining or propelling the ongoing growth of the two economies and where they are likely to rank in the global leagues—circa 2025. We also make the case that the next ten years will be marked by greater convergence rather than complementarity in the two economies. We then analyze the structure of trade and investment linkages between the two economies and argue that the coming years will see faster growth in investment rather than in trade linkages.

Chapter Two presents an overview of the opportunities and challenges that China poses for multinational companies, with a particular focus on those from India. The opportunities derive from the changing structure of the Chinese economy. Since China is not a niche economy, opportunities exist everywhere. Nonetheless, certain industry sectors offer higher-growth opportunities than do others. These include services of almost all types: industrial automation, solutions for energy efficiency, pollution control equipment and services, technologies for boosting agricultural productivity and addressing water scarcity, and, last but not least, most types of luxury goods. In this chapter we also examine the challenges pertaining to the "Indian mindset" regarding China, some important differences in the value systems of the two cultures, the omnipresent role of the government and the Communist Party in China, China's legal system, the vastness and diversity of China, the rapid pace of change, the differing priorities of large companies in China (mostly state-owned enterprises) versus those in India (mostly private-sector companies), intellectual property risks, managing talent, and building an institutional brand in China.

Chapter Three presents the evolutionary journey of Tata Consultancy Services (TCS) in China. TCS is India's largest company in the information technology (IT) sector. It is also a global giant, with a market value exceeding US$50 billion. TCS's experience in China highlights the centrality of home country advantages when entering another market (especially a brutally competitive one such as China) and of developing the company's China strategy from a wider "global" rather than a narrower "in-China-for-China" perspective. As TCS did, it is important to ask two key questions: What competitive advantages (such as technology, organizational capabilities, corporate reputation, and global relationships) from India or elsewhere can we leverage when we enter China? How will being in China make us stronger outside China—in India itself, in the Asia Pacific region, and globally? Designing the company's China strategy from such a global perspective can significantly reduce the risks of failure while boosting the potential value to be realized from a China presence.

Chapter Four presents the case study of Mahindra Tractors in China. A unit of the Mahindra & Mahindra Group, Mahindra Tractors is India's largest tractor company and, in terms of tractors sold, also the world's largest. Mahindra entered China in 2005 through a relatively small majority-owned joint venture (JV) and is determined to make China a second home. Mahindra was deliberate about treating the first JV as a learning initiative. In 2009, the company made its second key move—a much bigger JV, where also Mahindra holds a controlling stake. By 2012, Mahindra had a 9–10 percent share of China's tractor market. Mahindra's experience echoes several of the lessons from that of TCS. In addition, this case also highlights the centrality of experiential learning ("crossing the river by feeling the stones," in Chinese parlance) and of being deliberate rather than ad-hoc about important questions such as whether to go alone or via a JV and, if the answer is to do a JV, whether or not you need to have a controlling stake and how you will manage the relationship with the JV partner. Mahindra appears to have excelled at addressing all of these issues wisely.

Chapter Five presents the China journey of NIIT, India's (and Asia's) largest company in the business of training IT professionals. NIIT entered China in 1997, chose to go alone, and is today one of China's largest companies in this sector. Like TCS, NIIT has clearly benefited from India's global leadership in IT services. However, the unique aspect of the NIIT case study is how this company never took "no" as the final answer and, over time, has managed to become an almost indispensable and eagerly sought-after partner by various arms of the Chinese government at all levels—cities, provinces, and the central government. NIIT started out by trying to get licenses from city governments in Beijing and Shanghai to offer its two-to-three-year-long nondegree programs. Government officials were familiar with short-duration nondegree adult education courses as well as multiyear degree programs. However, they saw a multiyear nondegree educational program as too radical an idea. The Beijing city government said "no." However, the Shanghai government decided to take a chance by giving NIIT permission to set up just one center under tightly controlled conditions. NIIT made sure that this center would be extremely successful at creating outcomes that the city officials would love—creating trained IT professionals who were in high demand by employers, all at no cost to the city. Building on this toehold, NIIT moved on to much bigger partnerships with city and provincial governments and has more recently signed an agreement with the central government in Beijing to help build the human capital infrastructure on the island province of Hainan. The NIIT case also demonstrates the importance of openness to local innovation, even when it may lead the company to depart significantly from proven business models in the home country. NIIT invented the "NIIT Inside" model in China and has now taken this model to other countries—including India.

Chapter Six presents the story of how Tata Motors has developed a multibillion dollar revenue business in China, not by going directly from India to China, but by taking an indirect route—from India to the United Kingdom to China. Tata Motors did this by acquiring the British company Jaguar Land Rover (JLR) from Ford Motor Company in 2008. Unlike the IT sector, India does not enjoy a strong brand image in autos. On top of this, Tata Motors is a weak player in India's passenger car business. Thus, it is hard to imagine how Tata could hope to enter and succeed in China's car industry by taking the direct route from India to China. Instead, what Tata did was to drive into China indirectly by leveraging JLR's technological strength, strong brand image, and British heritage. We predict that, for Indian as well as Chinese companies, this type of indirect route will become one of the major strategic options over the coming decade. Mahindra is now contemplating entering China's SUV market via its South Korean subsidiary SsangYong. Wipro, another Indian company, has recently entered the branded consumer goods business in China via acquisitions in Singapore and Malaysia. On the Chinese side, examples include Geely's acquisition of Volvo, the Swedish car company, and Sany Heavy's acquisition of Putzmeister, the German concrete pumps company. Growing their businesses in India by leveraging the Swedish and German brands, products, and technologies should enable these companies to succeed in India at a much faster pace than entering directly from China.

In Chapter Seven, we present case studies on five Chinese companies (Lenovo, Haier, Huawei, Xinxing Heavy, and TBEA) that are not merely exporting to India but also have invested in R&D and/or manufacturing operations in the country. Lenovo competes in personal computers, Haier in home appliances, Huawei in telecom equipment, TBEA in high-voltage transformers, and Xinxing in steel pipes for potable water. These companies cover the gamut from branded consumer goods (Lenovo and Haier) to infrastructure equipment (Huawei, TBEA, and Xinxing). As these case studies illustrate, in both directions—from India to China and China to India—the economic relationship between the two countries is changing from largely trade to also include rapidly growing direct investment. They also point out that because China and India are two of the largest and fastest-growing emerging markets, both countries present brutal competition among not just domestic players but also those from the United States, Europe, Japan, and South Korea. The brutal competition implies that, just as with Indian companies in China, Chinese companies hoping to succeed in India need to design their India strategies from a global perspective rather than through just an "in-India-for-India" lens. Lenovo and Huawei bring out this conclusion most sharply.

The concluding Chapter Eight brings together the strategic lessons and guidelines that emerge for Indian companies eager to succeed in China. These strategic guidelines include being clear about the distinctive competencies—from the Indian operations or from a third country as in the case of Tata Motors and JLR—that the company will leverage as it enters China;

designing the company's China strategy with a global perspective rather than through an "in-China-for-China" lens; figuring out how to significantly reduce the risks of failure by starting out with a beachhead segment where the prospects for success are high and the company can begin to get traction without losing its shirt; being strategically astute regarding the important question of whether to partner or go alone and, in the case of a joint venture, how to identify the ideal partner and manage the ongoing relationship; treating government relationships at all levels as far more important in China than in any other market including India; being systematic about how to build product and institutional brands; and, above all, treating the company's China journey as a learning process. Irrespective of how thorough the company has been at its ex-ante analysis, in a market as different and dynamic as China, it is a certainty that there will be surprises. Being a rapid learner, as illustrated vividly by NIIT's journey in China, can increase the odds of success dramatically.

The sole agenda of some of the early travelers from India to China (such as Kumarajiva) and China to India (Fa Xian) was purely to learn from each other. We do not mean to suggest that today's business leaders should abandon more "mundane" goals such as revenues, profits, and shareholder value. We do believe, however, that businessmen and women who are rediscovering the Silk Road and who journey on it with a learning mindset are more likely to end up not just wiser but also more successful. We encourage you to think of China as not just a playground but also a school. Fortunes will be made or lost depending on not just how astute one is at designing long-term strategies but also how skillful one is at learning from direct experience.

Acknowledgments

No one works alone and no work is ever perfect. We are well aware that, like anything that has ever been written, this book also is a work in progress. While we are solely responsible for any and all weaknesses and limitations that remain, we are deeply grateful to many friends and colleagues who have helped shape our ideas and provided impetus for writing this book.

First and foremost, we would like to acknowledge Prakash Menon (president, NIIT China), Harish Chavan (until recently, president, Mahindra China), Prem Kumar (until recently, president, Sundaram Fasteners China), Bob Grace (president, Jaguar Land Rover China), N. Chandrasekaran, (CEO, Tata Consultancy Services), V. Rajanna (ex-country head, TCS China), William Hickey (until recently, CEO, Sealed Air Corporation), Li Xin (until recently, president, Sealed Air China), Shane Tedjerati (president, Global High Growth Regions, Honeywell Corporation), Viktor Sekmakas (executive vice president, PPG Industries), Rajeev Singh-Molares (president,

Asia-Pacific, Alcatel Lucent), Pierre Cohade (until recently, president, Asia-Pacific, Goodyear), and many other senior leaders of Indian and Western multinationals who generously shared their time and views regarding what it takes to succeed in China's vast, diverse, and dynamic market and the role that China and India play in their companies' global strategies.

We are also grateful to the many executives of Chinese companies who helped us understand the evolution of their companies' strategies in India. In particular, we would like to acknowledge Guo Ping, deputy chairman of the Board and Rotating CEO, Huawei Technologies; Zhang Ruimin, chairman and CEO, Haier Group; and Zeng Ming, chief strategy officer, Alibaba Group, for helping us better understand their companies' evolving global strategies and how they see India's role in these strategies.

We have also benefited from extensive discussions with key players in the India-China relationship, including Nirupama Rao, who just retired as India's Ambassador to the U.S. after earlier responsibilities as India's Foreign Secretary and Ambassador to China; S. Jaishankar, who recently moved to Washington, DC as India's Ambassador to the U.S. from Beijing where he was Ambassador to China; and Zhang Yan, until recently China's Ambassador to India. We owe a particular debt of gratitude to Anand Raman, editor-at-large at *Harvard Business Review*, who has been a good friend and intellectual soul mate on the subject of global strategy. Thank you all for educating us.

Kathe Sweeney, executive editor at Jossey-Bass/Wiley, has been a central player in helping us launch this project and in pushing us to get it completed without too much delay. Given her role as an editor for one of the world's leading publishers, her enthusiasm and guidance have been particularly important in bringing this project to fruition.

Thank you all for giving us your time, friendship, care, and the benefit of your insights. While we alone are responsible for the deficiencies that remain, we hope that you will be proud of the final product.

Anil K. Gupta, Girija Pande, Haiyan Wang
Beijing, New Delhi, Singapore, Washington, DC

1

Asia's Best-Kept Secret

Growing Economic Ties Between India and China

On March 15, 2013, Mr. Li Keqiang was elected by the Communist Party Congress as premier, the second most important position in the Chinese government after General Secretary and President Xi Jinping. Two months later, Premier Li embarked on his maiden official visit outside China. The first stop on his tour? A three-day visit to India. Hopping over to India so early in his term was a clear signal of China's foreign policy priorities. As the premier remarked upon his arrival in New Delhi: "We are one-third of the world's total population and our interactions attract the world. Without doubt, China-India relations are [among the] most important global relations."[1]

As is true for many neighbors, the relationship between India and China remains full of tensions—both economic as well as geopolitical—which we discuss later in this chapter.

These tensions are unlikely to ease any time soon. Yet there are good reasons to predict that the economic ties between the two countries will continue to strengthen and, by 2025, will be among the ten most important bilateral ties between any two countries in the world.

Even if the Chinese and Indian economies were to grow at only a 5–6 percent annual rate over the next ten years, by 2025 they would rank as the largest and fourth-largest economies in the world, the other two being those of the United States and Japan.[2] Both countries have also become springboards for the emergence of global champions across a range of industries from technology (Tata Consultancy Services, Infosys, Huawei, and Lenovo) to heavy manufacturing (Tata Motors, Mahindra, Geely, and Chery) to fast-moving consumer goods (Godrej and Shuanghui). Given the size and growth rate of the two economies, growing numbers of Chinese and Indian companies with global ambitions have little choice but to look across the Himalayas and think of their neighbor as one of the world's largest markets sitting right next door.

To date, economic ties between India and China have been dominated by trade rather than investment. Bilateral trade between the two grew from less than $3 billion in 2000 to $69 billion in 2012—an annual growth rate of almost 30 percent, significantly faster than the 19.4 percent and 19.2 percent annual growth rates, respectively, in China's and India's trades with the rest of the world, or the 9.2 percent growth rate in world trade.[3] In contrast, the stock of foreign direct investment has been small. At the end of 2012, the stock of Chinese investment in India added up to only about $800 million.

The stock of Indian investment in China was also equally small—about $500 million.[4] However, the picture is changing rapidly. India's Mahindra Group is currently the fifth-largest tractor manufacturer in China, with a market share of about 9–10 percent. It aims to move up to a number three position within the next five years. Tata Motors' Jaguar Land Rover subsidiary (JLR) has been the fastest-growing luxury auto seller in China over the last five years. In November 2012, JLR established a 50:50 joint venture (JV) with China's Chery. The partners are investing more than RMB 10 billion in a new manufacturing plant and R&D facilities in Changshu, near Shanghai, which are expected to go onstream in 2014. China's Huawei has had its second largest R&D center in Bangalore since the late 1990s. Huawei currently employs over five thousand people in India and has also started manufacturing operations in the country to make telecom hardware. Haier, the home appliance giant, currently manufactures refrigerators at a plant in Pune, India. Given its robust growth in the Indian market, it is now planning to expand its manufacturing base in the country. These are just some of the new developments presently under way in both countries.

This book is targeted at the leaders of both Indian and Chinese multinationals for whom the other country could be a supplier, a customer, a competitor, and a partner and who view their Himalayan neighbor with a sense of mystery and perhaps trepidation. It should also be of high interest to policy makers in both countries (since they serve as important gatekeepers) as well as to leaders of multinational corporations in the United States, Europe, Japan, South Korea, and other countries with operations in both countries. Growing integration

3

between India and China will offer new opportunities as well as new competitive challenges to their companies. It is important for them to know what's afoot.

In this chapter, we discuss the evolving ties between India and China. Although our primary focus is on economic linkages, we begin with a discussion of the historical ties between the two civilizations, the recent history of geopolitical tensions between them, and how their citizens view each other. This multifaceted examination of cross-country ties is important because economic relations are not only embedded in and influenced by cultural linkages, personal attitudes, and geopolitical relationships but, in turn, also shape them.

Subsequent chapters discuss the potential opportunities that Indian companies could pursue in China and the challenges that they are likely to face. We also present detailed case studies of some of the pioneering Indian companies that have made a long-term commitment to China and are beginning to see that commitment pay off. These case studies may inspire and offer lessons to other Indian companies contemplating a move into China. Rounding out the story, we also include a chapter on corporate moves in the other direction—that is, the entry of Chinese companies into India. We close by offering a China-focused roadmap for Indian companies.

THE HISTORICAL BACKDROP

But for a brief border war in 1962 and the subsequent tensions that remain alive, China and India have enjoyed a harmonious relationship going back more than two thousand years. Unlike, say, the relationship between China and Japan, there is no fundamental fault line between the Indians and the Chinese. Yes, there is wariness (on the part of the Indians) and a degree of disdain (on the part of the Chinese). However, there is no emotional dislike between the two peoples.

In ancient times, the ties that brought China and India together were religious and intellectual as well as economic. Serious cultural interactions began in the fourth and fifth centuries A.D. when Indian and Chinese scholars traveled to each other's countries and played a key role in bringing Buddhism to China. Two of the key players were the Chinese monk Fa Xian and the Indian scholar Kumarajiva. Fa Xian visited India in the early part of the fifth century, stayed there for ten years and, upon his return to China, translated many Sanskrit and Buddhist texts into Chinese. Kumarajiva collected and translated many important Buddhist texts into Chinese at a large Buddhist complex in Chang-an (today's Xian). He lived there until his death in 413 A.D. The scholarly exchanges continued for many centuries, with people such as the Indians Dharmakshema and Bodhidharma and the Chinese Fa Hein, Xuan Zhang, and I Ching taking the Silk Road to share ideas with each other's cultures.

In the eighth century, an Indian scientist was appointed by China as the president of its Board of Astronomy. And the famous fifteenth century Chinese admiral Zheng He (who reportedly had a more impressive fleet than that of Christopher Columbus) visited India often and played an important role in expanding trade links between the two countries.

Although cultural exchanges remained dormant during the colonial period in both countries, the underlying warmth endured. In the early twentieth century, the poet and Nobel laureate Rabindranath Tagore visited China and was welcomed with love and respect. Following both countries' independence from occupying powers, the 1950s promised to usher in an era of exceptional warmth in the relationship. India was one of the first countries to end formal ties with Taiwan and recognize the PRC as the legitimate government of China. Alas, the Sino-Indian war of 1962—rooted in border disputes and India's decision to give sanctuary to the Dalai Lama—brought an end to any further talk of "*Hindi Chini Bhai Bhai*" (Indians and Chinese are brothers).

Indians remain bitter about the war to this day. Across the Himalayas, however, the Chinese soon found themselves consumed by events far more dramatic and much closer to home—the Cultural Revolution. For the average Chinese citizen, the outside world ceased to matter and the war with India receded from memory. In 1976, the cultural revolution came to an abrupt end with the deaths of both Mao Zedong and Zhou Enlai. As the new leaders started experimenting with opening up and reforms, China met India again—through films such as *Awaara* and *Do Bigha Zameen*. Following the oppressiveness of the Cultural Revolution, these films were like a breath of fresh air. Here is a personal account from Haiyan Wang, a Chinese and a coauthor of this book, who lived through this period.

Awaara—A Cultural and Emotional Landmark for Millions of Chinese

Awaara hoon, Awaara hoon ...
Ya gardish mein hoon
Aasman ka tara hoon ...

Hum this song today to any Chinese man or woman born in the mid-1960s or earlier, no matter in what rank of position or field of work, and the chances are pretty high that he or she will hum back. It's the title song from Raj Kapoor's 1951 movie *Awaara*. Screened in 1977 in cinemas across China, *Awaara* swept across the country like a spring breeze melting winter's frozen ground, a breathtaking experience for millions of Chinese people.

Humming the songs from this film was the coolest and trendiest thing back then. I remember huddling around a borrowed cassette player with a dozen of my middle school classmates. We played the songs "*Ghar Aaya Mera Pardesi*" and "*Ab Raat Guzarne Wali Hai*" over and over again for hours to learn to sing them, so that we could perform on stage in school.

The year 1977 was at the end of the cultural revolution and the dawn of China's opening and reform. Having been allowed to see only a small number of revolutionary films during the cultural revolution, we were blown away by the artistry, the imagery, the radiant beauty of the main characters, Raj and Rita, the songs, and the sensual scenes. For the first time, watching a movie was not about getting a lesson in communism but about letting your imagination run.

> Oh World! I am devastated,
> but I sing songs of happiness.
> My chest is full of wounds,
> but my carefree gaze laughs …

So sings Raj, the vagabond. Having endured the anguish of life and hardship of poverty like Raj did, we found it refreshing and uplifting to find in Raj an unyielding free spirit and romantic passion.

Before there was Hollywood in China, there was Bollywood. It was this Indian film that first gave millions of Chinese people a window on the outside world—a world that was not about ideology or revolution, but about the pursuit of freedom, love, and humanity.

—Haiyan Wang

The Chinese fascination with Indian culture remains alive and well. With growing affluence, urban Chinese are once again turning to Buddhism in increasing numbers. As well, the practice of yoga is spreading to every corner of China. There is even the distinct possibility that Bollywood films and songs may make a comeback. *Life of Pi*—set in India, although not a Bollywood film—was extremely popular throughout China.

During the summer of 2012, we were pleasantly surprised to find dozens of Chinese couples dancing to the tunes of a Bollywood song in the public square in Xian. A Chinese studio is even working on a cross-cultural Chinese and Indian film due for commercial release in late 2014.

Might *Gold Struck* Strike Gold?

In August 2013, Hong Kong–based Light House Productions announced that they will shortly begin shooting *Gold Struck*, a cross-cultural film complete with Chinese martial arts and Bollywood songs and dances. The film is expected to be the story of two Indian and Chinese research students who become friends at an American university and then embark on a time-travel adventure that takes them back to 220 B.C. in China's Qin Dynasty era.

The film will be directed by Tony Cheung and Cory Yeun and feature dialogue in English, Mandarin, and Hindi. It will be shot in the United States, China, and India and released in all three countries as well as other markets such as Australia, Canada, and the United Kingdom, which have high numbers of both Chinese and Indian immigrants. Light House is collaborating with Gayathiri Batra, an Indian media executive. Cindy Shyu, Light House's CEO, explained that her motivation for making this film originated with the realization that, although Chinese audiences have long been interested in Indian films and dance, they currently have little opportunity to experience Indian cinema. Because the film is being produced by a Chinese company, it will not be considered an import and thus will be free from import restrictions on foreign films.[5]

GEOPOLITICAL TENSIONS: AN IRRITANT BUT NOT A SHOW STOPPER

Ask any observer of India and China—in the government, the industry, academia, or the media—to describe the relationship between the two neighbors, and it is a near certainty that "trust deficit" will emerge as one of the top two observations. Geopolitical tensions are the root cause of the ongoing lack of trust.

Unresolved border disagreements and China's enduring support for Pakistan are the two biggest factors behind the geopolitical tensions.[6] Other contributing factors include India's hosting of the Dalai Lama as an "honored guest" and growing competition between the two countries in the Indian Ocean region.[7] It is our contention that, although all of these are significant irritants for both sides, none poses any foreseeable danger to a more rapid and deeper economic collaboration between the two countries. In fact, deeper economic engagement, especially via direct investments, holds the prospect of helping both sides mitigate and perhaps resolve the geopolitical tensions in due course.

Consider border disputes, the single most contentious issue. India and China share a 2,500-mile border. Ever since India's independence in 1947 and the formation of the People's Republic of China in 1949, the two countries have never agreed on the boundaries that divide them. To the north of India, China controls a vast area that India claims to be part of its territory. And on India's northeastern frontier, the Indian state of Arunachal Pradesh is claimed by China as its South Tibet. After the 1962 war, both sides started placing observers and troops along the line of actual control. Until 1987, daily exchanges of gunfire were routine. That year, the two countries even came close to another war.

The December 1988 visit to China by Rajiv Gandhi served as a turning point. This was the first visit to China by an Indian prime minister since the 1954 trip by Jawaharlal Nehru. Gandhi's visit resulted in an agreement to seek a peaceful and mutually acceptable solution. India and China would set up a joint working group on the boundary question and hold annual consultations between their foreign ministers. The two sides also agreed to establish direct air links and cooperation in economic and scientific matters.

Twenty-five years later, the two countries are no closer to resolving the boundary disputes than they were in 1988. Each also routinely accuses the other of incursions along the line of control. From time to time, China also starts stapling (rather than stamping) its visa on the passports of Indian nationals from the states of Jammu and Kashmir and Arunachal Pradesh—a practice that infuriates India, whose Foreign Affairs Ministry will not accept the stapled visas as legitimate.

In 2012, China began issuing new passports to its citizens that included a map showing various disputed territories to be part of China. Immediately thereafter, the Indian government started using a new visa stamp that included its own version of the map of India.

While these skirmishes continue, it is critical to remember that for almost twenty-five years the guns have been silent. Leaders of both countries appear to believe that the most important agenda for them is economic development. This requires peace on the borders. As Mrs. Nirupama Rao, India's Ambassador to the United States—and former foreign secretary as well as former ambassador to China—noted in a 2012 speech at the Hudson Institute: "The foremost task of India's foreign policy is to enable the domestic transformation of India ... This requires us to work for a supportive external environment that is peaceful, thus enabling us to concentrate on our growth and development."[8]

President Xi Jinping's remarks after a 2013 meeting with Prime Minister Manmohan Singh on the sidelines of the BRICS (Brazil, Russia, India, China, and South Africa) summit in Durban, South Africa, echo a very similar viewpoint: "China and India should broaden exchanges and cooperation between their armed forces and deepen mutual military and security trust ... [Both sides] should continue to safeguard peace in their border areas and prevent the issue from affecting bilateral relations ... [Both sides] have a similar mission to boost their social and economic development ... in an important period of strategic opportunities."[9]

Consider also the views expressed by Premier Li and Prime Minister Singh in a joint address during the former's visit to India in May 2013:

> Premier Li: "We don't deny that there are problems between the two sides. We need to improve border related mechanisms and make them more efficient. Both Mr. Singh and I believe there are far more common interests than differences between our two sides. We need to confront issues with a broad mind and tackle them in a mature way."

> Prime Minister Singh: "[India and China] have agreed that our special representatives will meet soon to continue discussions seeking an early agreement on a framework for a fair, reasonable and mutually acceptable boundary settlement. Peace and tranquility on our border has to be preserved."[10]

Entirely consistent with these viewpoints, a 2011 U.S. Defense Department study, based on confidential interviews with policy advisors in both India and China, summed up the situation as follows: "Indian and Chinese officials and analysts recognize that despite … tensions between them, they have strong incentives to keep the relationship stable. Both countries confront serious economic development and domestic stability issues at home, and both countries are trying to promote peaceful security environments that are not hostile to their rise in power."[11]

Interestingly, the contentious issue of Pakistan also forces China and India to maintain stable and peaceful relations with each other. Although it is undoubtedly true that friendship with Pakistan gives China some leverage over India, the future stability of Pakistan is a major and shared concern for both China and India. Should Pakistan's internal situation worsen or its nuclear arsenal fall into the hands of extremists, that would be a nightmarish scenario for both countries.

There are four reasons why we believe that the odds favor a stable and peaceful rather than a turbulent relationship between India and China. First, as already noted, political leaders in both countries realize that their nations face extremely large opportunities for economic and social development. Realizing these opportunities requires peace on the borders. Second, leaders on both sides openly accept their mutual destiny as two of the world's leading superpowers by the middle of the century. Thus they have little choice but to keep searching for a way to coexist amicably and join as responsible large powers in the governance of global institutions. Given also their rapidly growing economies, they have much to gain from stronger economic ties.

Third, two of China's immediate neighbors (Japan and South Korea) already have defense treaties with the United States. Others (such as Philippines and Vietnam) are moving in that direction. India too is developing an increasingly close relationship with the United States. A serious deterioration in the India-China relationship will significantly increase the likelihood of a formal treaty between India and the United States. Given the existing global rivalry between China and the United States, it is more advantageous for China if India remains a relatively neutral player rather than becoming solidly aligned with the United States.

Last but not least, India is boosting its defense capabilities aggressively through both internal efforts as well as procurement from and technological collaboration with the United States, Russia, France, and the United Kingdom. These efforts include building and/or acquiring nuclear weapons, stealth aircraft, nuclear-powered submarines, aircraft carriers, as well as missiles capable of reaching almost anywhere in China. As with the cold war between the United States and the U.S.S.R., this build-up is creating a détente whereby neither side could risk starting a hot war with the other.

In light of these factors, we believe that there are solid reasons to accept at face value President Xi's public statements after his March 2013 meeting with Indian leaders in Durban, South Africa: "The border question is a complex issue left from history and solving the issue won't be easy. However, as long as we keep up friendly consultations, we can eventually arrive at a fair, reasonable and mutually acceptable settlement. Pending the final settlement of the boundary question .... we should harness each other's comparative strengths and expand win-win cooperation in infrastructure, mutual investment and other areas."[12]

PEOPLE'S ATTITUDES: GROWING WARINESS AMIDST MUTUAL RESPECT

Since the turn of the twenty-first century, growing numbers of Indian and Chinese tourists have been travelling to and getting a direct exposure to each other's country. Since 2005, the numbers of Chinese tourists visiting India and Indian tourists visiting China have each grown at an annual rate of about 25 percent, well above the 15-percent and 11-percent growth rates in worldwide outbound tourism from China and India, respectively. In absolute terms, however, the numbers remain small. The 600,000 Indian tourists who visited China in 2012 accounted for less than 1 percent of the more than 60 million visitors to China that year. Similarly, the 150,000 Chinese tourists who visited India in 2012 made up about 2.5 percent of the 6.6 million visitors to India that year.

It's important to note that this growing mutual exposure has not resulted in a more positive attitude toward or growing trust in each other. If anything, the result has been quite the contrary. Yes, the two peoples have enormous respect for each other. Indians think of the Chinese as extremely disciplined and driven. In turn, the Chinese think of the Indians as very creative and very smart. Nonetheless, on both sides, people are more wary of each other now than they were in 2006. Results from ongoing surveys conducted by the Pew Global Attitudes Project are telling. Figure 1.1 provides trend data for 2006–2012 regarding the percentage of Indians and Chinese who hold a favorable attitude toward the other country.

As Figure 1.1 tells us, in 2006, there were far more Indians with a favorable attitude toward China than there were Chinese with a favorable attitude toward India. By 2012, however, both numbers had declined significantly—to 23 percent. As a benchmark, note that, in 2012, both the Indians and the Chinese hold a much more favorable attitude toward the United

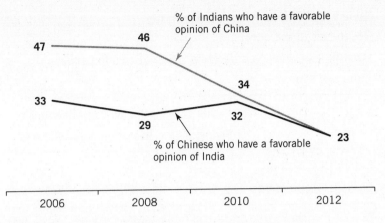

% of Indians who have a favorable opinion of China

47 46

34

33

29 32

% of Chinese who have a favorable opinion of India

23

2006   2008   2010   2012

Figure 1.1 Growing Wariness Among the Two Peoples

Source: Pew Global Attitudes Project.

States (41 percent and 43 percent, respectively) than they do toward each other.

Table 1.1 contains results from survey data regarding how the Indians and the Chinese look at the relationship between their two countries. Indians appear to be more wary of the Chinese than vice versa. As of 2012, more Chinese saw the relationship as one of cooperation rather than hostility (39 percent versus 24 percent, respectively). In contrast, fewer Indians saw the relationship as cooperative rather than hostile (23 percent versus 24 percent, respectively).

What factors lie behind this growing wariness? Our analysis and interviews suggest that Indians' growing disenchantment with China stems from three major factors:

1. *Unresolved border tensions.* India lost the 1962 war with China. As is nearly always the case, the loser has a tougher time forgetting the past than the winner does. Among adult

Table 1.1   A Mixed Motive Relationship
Responses to the question:
Overall, how would you describe the relationship between India and China?

	One of Cooperation	One of Hostility	Neither/Don't Know/Refused
Indian Respondents	23%	24%	53%
Chinese Respondents	39%	24%	37%

Note: India data from 4,018 face-to-face interviews representing 86 percent of the country's urban and rural adults. China data from 3,177 face-to-face interviews representing 64 percent of the country's urban and rural adults (with the caveat that the sample was disproportionately urban).
Source: Pew Global Attitudes Project, Spring 2012.

Chinese today, very few are aware that there has ever been a war between China and India. In contrast, almost all Indians seem to know about the war. What makes Indians particularly wary is China's all-weather friendship with Pakistan, a country with which India has fought numerous wars and whose terrorists were responsible for the Mumbai massacre in 2008. Most Indians also believe that China is gaining the upper hand in terms of economic and military relationships with its other neighbors such as Sri Lanka, Myanmar, and Nepal, thereby encircling India with a "string of pearls."

2. *India's large and growing trade deficit with China*. Although oil imports are the single biggest contributor to India's ballooning trade deficit, the imbalance in trade with China has become a growing challenge for the country. Our analysis, presented

later in this chapter, suggests that India's weakness in manufacturing is the primary reason for the trade deficit with China. Yet government ministers as well as media articles in India attribute the trade deficit largely to trade barriers erected by the Chinese government.

3. *Growing economic disparity between the two countries.* As recently as 1980, China and India were equally poor and at near parity in terms of GDP and per capita income. Over the last thirty years, however, China has raced ahead. In 2012, China's GDP was over four times that of India. Two factors have contributed to this gap. First, India did not launch major economic reforms until 1991, fully thirteen years later than the launch of China's reforms in 1978. Second, even though India has been the world's second fastest-growing large economy after China, the power of compounding has made a difference. The growing economic gap between the two has made Indians increasingly envious of their northern neighbor.

In turn, the growing wariness of the Chinese toward India stems from a somewhat different set of factors.

1. *Disdain for India's weak infrastructure and seeming chaos.* When Chinese travelers visit India, they are taken aback by the stark difference between the first-world infrastructure in most Chinese cities and the still third-world infrastructure even in Tier 1 cities such as Delhi and Mumbai. Added to this, given their government's obsession with order, Chinese visitors cannot fathom how Indian authorities could permit the chaos that seems to prevail on almost any Indian road—disorganized

traffic, two- and three-wheelers intermingling with cars and trucks, and the common sight of cows sharing the road with everybody.

2. *Materiality versus spiritualism.* It is widely accepted that contemporary Chinese society is one of the most materialistic in the world. More than half a century of communist rule succeeded in converting most Chinese into atheists. Although there is now a growing search for spirituality, especially among the urban affluent, it is still in the early stages. Thus, when the Chinese assess other countries, the most important criterion is "How well off are you?" On this measure India comes up short, and the country's spirituality doesn't quite make up for its economic backwardness. As a result, the Chinese have a mixed attitude toward India. Chinese media routinely lauds India's creativity and global power in software and IT services. Indians have also outpaced the Chinese in the race for global CEO positions at blue-chip Western corporations, such as Deutsche Bank, Citigroup, PepsiCo, Diageo, and Microsoft. Thus the Chinese have high respect for India's IT sector and tend to regard Indians as well-educated and brainy. At the same time, they view the Indian government as, by and large, not particularly competent.

3. *The U.S.-India Civil Nuclear Agreement.* In 2005, India's Prime Minister Manmohan Singh and U.S. President George W. Bush signed a framework agreement for the transfer of civilian nuclear technology and fuel. In 2008, the framework agreement became law on both sides and had also been ratified by the world's Nuclear Suppliers Group. This agreement made India the only known country with nuclear weapons that had not signed the Non-Proliferation Treaty but was still able to engage

openly in nuclear commerce with the rest of the world. The U.S. government positioned this agreement as part of a broader strategic partnership aimed at accelerating India's emergence as a superpower. Since then, the geopolitical alliance between the United States and India has grown stronger. The Chinese media have portrayed these moves as designed to "contain" China.

To sum up, in our view the wariness between India and China is likely to persist for some time. As foreign direct investment ramps up and Indians and Chinese find themselves working for each other, this will help rebuild liking and trust. Real transformation in mutual trust, however, will have to wait until the border disagreements begin to be resolved. In the meantime, governments, academia, and media should explore all possible opportunities to encourage mutual visits by policy makers at not just the national but also local level, as well as the exchange of scholars and students. At the very least, ongoing dialogue through these channels will reduce the likelihood of a further worsening in the existing low level of trust.

CHINA AND INDIA IN 2025

During the dozen years from 2000–2012, China and India have been the world's two fastest growing economies (see Figure 1.2). The fact remains, however, that both economies have slowed down considerably during 2011–2013 (see Figure 1.3). Compared to its twelve-year average of 10.2 percent a year, China's economy is expected to grow by about

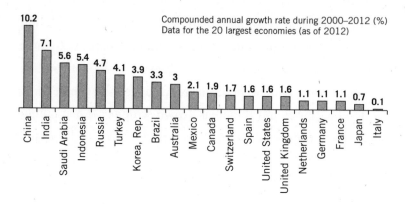

Figure 1.2   The World's Two Fastest-Growing Economies

Source: The World Bank.

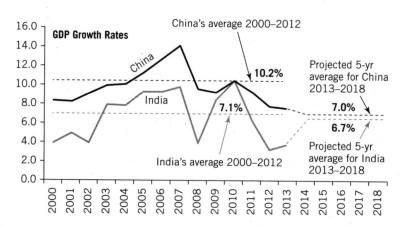

Figure 1.3   Recent Slowdown but Expected to Maintain Rapid Growth

Source: The World Bank (for 2000–2012) and IMF (for 2013–2018 projections).

7.5 percent in 2013. For India, compared to its twelve-year average of 7.1 percent, the economy is expected to grow by only 3.8 percent in 2013.

The slowdown raises an important question: Is the China-India growth story over? The answer lies in an analysis of the factors behind the slowdown.

Take China. There is enough evidence to conclude that the slowdown in China is structural and that the era of over 10 percent annual growth is over for good. However, even at a much slower 5- to 7-percent annual growth rate, China will overtake the United States to become the world's largest economy by 2025 (see Table 1.2 for trend data and our predictions about the world's top twelve economies in 2025).

The structural slowdown is a result of the fact that China can no longer sustain economic growth fueled by massive expansion in fixed asset investment, exports, and a growing supply of cheap labor. In 2012, investment reached close to 50 percent of GDP and was financed largely by credit taken on by local governments and state-owned enterprises. Public debt now stands at about 200 percent of GDP. Counting off-budget spending by local governments, China's fiscal deficit has reached almost 10 percent of GDP. These figures are no longer sustainable.

Consider also the trend in exports and labor supply. From 2000–2012, China's exports grew at average annual rate of 19.4 percent relative to a growth rate in world exports of 9.2 percent. As a result, China's share of world exports grew from 3.9 percent in 2000 to 11.1 percent in 2012.[13] If these trends were to continue, by 2025 China's share of world exports would be

Table 1.2 World's Top Twelve Economies

2000	2012	2020	2025
1 United States	1 United States	1 United States	*1 China*
2 Japan	*2 China*	*2 China*	2 United States
3 Germany	3 Japan	3 Japan	3 Japan
4 United Kingdom	4 Germany	4 Germany	*4 India*
5 France	5 France	*5 India*	5 Germany
6 China	6 United Kingdom	6 Brazil	6 Brazil
7 Italy	7 Brazil	7 France	7 Russia
8 Canada	8 Russia	8 Russia	8 France
9 Brazil	9 Italy	9 United Kingdom	9 United Kingdom
10 Mexico	*10 India*	10 Italy	10 Italy
11 Spain	11 Canada	11 Canada	11 Canada
12 South Korea	12 Australia	12 Australia	12 Indonesia
13 *India*			

Note: For 2000 and 2012, based on data from The World Bank. For 2020 and 2025, projections are based on the following assumptions about GDP growth rates: China 6 percent; India 6 percent; Brazil 3 percent; Russia 3 percent; Indonesia 6 percent; other economies 2.5 percent. For the BRIC economies and Indonesia, we also assume an average 2-percent higher inflation than in the developed economies.
Source: China India Institute analysis.

35 percent. This is simply impossible unless the large importing countries (such as the United States, Europe, and India) decide to commit economic suicide, which is unlikely. Clearly, from here on, China's exports would grow at about half the

pace of that over the last decade. In terms of labor supply, during 2000–2010 China's labor pool grew at an average annual rate of about 1 percent. Since 2011, it has stopped growing—an after-effect of the government's one-child policy. From 2015 onward, it will start declining at the rate of about 0.5 percent per year.[14]

A slowdown in China's economic growth does not, however, mean economic collapse. China is still a developing country with tremendous opportunities for ongoing productivity growth. Its infrastructure is excellent, its savings rate high, and its people increasingly better educated. Thus the prospects remain high that China will be able to sustain economic growth at a 5- to 7-percent rate for the next decade or more.[15] As the IMF noted in its most recent *World Economic Outlook*:

> Growth in China has been on a decelerating path… . Imbalances between private consumption and investment have intensified, even as the economy's external imbalances have narrowed. A decisive move to contain these imbalances may be accompanied by lower medium-term growth than achieved by China in recent decades, but this is a trade-off worth making, since it is likely to usher in permanently higher living standards than under the extension of the status-quo.[16]

Table 1.3 summarizes the key factors that have driven rapid economic growth in China, the primary reasons behind the current slowdown, and the key drivers that will keep China's

Table 1.3 China's Growth Drivers and Constraints

Primary Drivers of GDP Growth During 2000–2010	Growing labor force
	Very high rate of savings and investment
	Rapidly growing urbanization
	Rapid advances in infrastructure
	Emergence as the world's manufacturing powerhouse
	Rapid growth in exports
Key Factors Behind the Current Slowdown	Overinvestment in infrastructure
	End of growth in size of labor force
	Rapidly rising wages resulting in slowdown in growth of exports
Expected Growth Drivers 2014–2025	Ongoing urbanization
	Productivity growth driven by rising automation rather than cheap and growing migrant labor pool
	Growth in services sector
	Moderation in oil prices (a key import commodity)

economy growing at a still-robust annual growth rate of 5 to 7 percent over the next decade.

The factors behind India's slowdown are a mirror image of those in the case of China. Although China's challenges stem from too much investment and too little consumption (relative to GDP), India's stem from too little investment and too much consumption (see Figure 1.4).

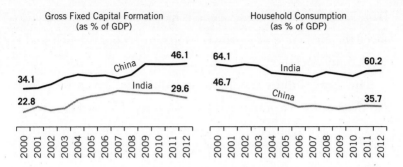

Figure 1.4 China Is Investment Led; India Is Consumption Led
Source: The World Bank; China India Institute analysis.

The slowdown in investment has been particularly sharp since 2009, when the ruling Congress Party and its coalition partners returned to power. Owing to a number of factors (coalition politics, a barrage of corruption scandals, and weak leadership), policy making has been mired in near paralysis. As a result, the leaders have failed to make the needed short- to medium-term trade-offs among competing goals (economic growth, protecting the environment, and providing economic security to the weakest segments of society). Inadequate investment in infrastructure and factories has resulted in supply-side bottlenecks and, as a direct spillover, higher inflation. Driven by its mission to keep inflation under control, the central bank has kept interest rates high. These in turn have further discouraged investment—creating a vicious cycle.

Like China, India is also one of the world's major oil importers. However, unlike China, India is very weak in manufacturing. As a result, India has been unable to balance its large import bill with an equally large export base. The large and growing trade deficit has meant that India also faces the challenge of a growing current account deficit and a weakening currency.

In short, India's economic slowdown is driven by policy paralysis rather than structural constraints. The saving grace is that, time and again, Indian governments have tended to undertake major economic reforms only when confronted with a crisis. That is the situation now. During 2013, the government has launched a series of reforms including a sharp relaxation in the constraints on foreign direct investment in a number of industries, approval of a large number of backlogged investment projects, and plans to open up the banking sector to new entrants, both domestic and foreign. At the time of this writing, we believe that the pace of reforms will continue. The next round of national elections is due by May 2014. The leading opposition (Bharatiya Janata Party) appears even more committed to economic reforms than the Congress Party.

The IMF's most recent report forecasts that, during 2013–2018, India's GDP is likely to grow at an average annual rate of 6.7 percent.[17] *In short, notwithstanding the slowdown, China and India are expected to remain the world's two fastest-growing large economies for the near future.* As indicated earlier in Table 1.2, our own analysis suggests that, even if India's GDP were to grow at only a 5- to 6-percent growth rate (plus inflation at a 2- to 3-percent higher rate than in the rich economies), by 2025, it would become the world's fourth-largest economy, ahead of Germany and only slightly behind Japan.

Table 1.4 summarizes the key factors behind India's rapid economic growth over the last decade and the recent

Table 1.4 India's Growth Drivers and Constraints

Primary Drivers of GDP Growth During 2000–2010	Growing labor force
	Very high rate of savings
	Growing urbanization
	Better infrastructure (especially in telecommunications)
	Emergence as the world's information technology services powerhouse
Key Factors Behind the Current Slowdown	Policy paralysis leading to underinvestment and supply bottlenecks in mining, energy, and infrastructure
	Growing current account deficit due primarily to rapidly rising imports of oil and coal
	Inflationary pressures, which led the central bank to drive up interest rates
Expected Growth Drivers 2014–2025	Young population resulting in continued growth in labor force
	Rapid growth in urbanization
	Rapid improvements in infrastructure
	Faster growth of the manufacturing sector
	Diffusion of broadband internet access, resulting in rapid improvements in literacy and access to financial services
	Moderation in energy prices (a major import commodity)

slowdown, and the reasons why the slowdown is likely to be temporary rather than structural.

THINK CONVERGENCE, NOT COMPLEMENTARITY

China and India are also mirror opposites of each other in terms of the structure of their economies (see Figure 1.5).

For China, industry accounts for the biggest share of its GDP. For India, it is services. This contrast has led many observers to argue that the two economies have complementary strengths. We disagree. The "services" sector is made up of many different industries, including defense, financial services, telecommunications, air transportation, hotels, information technology (IT), and so forth. It is true that India is a global leader in IT services and much stronger than China. However, IT services comprise just a small share of India's

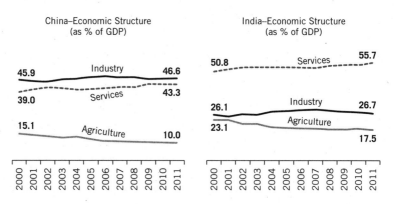

Figure 1.5   China and India: Economic Structure
Source: UNCTAD; China India Institute analysis.

GDP—about 5 percent. The reason why India's economy appears to be stronger in services is not because its overall service sector is necessarily stronger than China's but because its manufacturing sector is much weaker than China's.

Looking ahead, we anticipate that the next ten years will see a growing convergence in the two economies. As India starts investing more aggressively in infrastructure, its manufacturing sector will become much stronger. The rise of the manufacturing sector will also be aided by India's growing scale, its strong engineering skills, and labor costs that are lower than China's.

Across the mountains, we anticipate that, over the next decade, China will become much stronger in services than it currently is. The bulk of the development in China's services sector will take place on the eastern coast. This is the most developed region of China; it has the highest education levels and also, not coincidentally, the highest wages. As manufacturing migrates to central China, the east coast will focus increasingly on services and knowledge-intensive industries. The Shanghai Free Trade Zone set up in September 2013 and aimed at liberalizing the country's financial sector is just one of several services sector–oriented initiatives currently under way in China.[18]

The emerging convergence between the two economies means that Chinese and Indian policy makers as well as business leaders will need to think increasingly in terms of a multidimensional engagement with each other. Such engagement will encompass not just trade but also investment in each other's countries as well as partnerships to pursue opportunities in third countries.

CHINA-INDIA TRADE: EXPLOSIVE GROWTH BUT GROWING TENSIONS

The story of trade between China and India is one of explosive growth accompanied by underlying tensions. Table 1.5 presents data on the two countries' trade with each other as well as with other economies.

These data reveal several important trends. First, India's trade has grown at almost the same explosive pace as China's (19.2 percent and 19.4 percent, respectively). Second, with some exceptions, for both China and India trade with emerging economies has grown faster than trade with the developed economies. Third, from the perspective of both China and India, their trade with each other has grown faster than their trade with any other country. The 29.7-percent growth rate in bilateral trade between China and India is more than three times as fast as the 9.2-percent growth rate in world trade during this period.

In 2012, China was India's second-largest trading partner, after the United Arab Emirates. In turn, India was China's twelfth-largest and fastest-growing trading partner. During their meeting in May 2013, Premier Li Keqiang and Prime Minister Manmohan Singh set a goal of growing the bilateral trade between the two countries to US$100 billion by 2015. In light of historical trends, the odds of achieving this goal appear to be reasonable. These data also reinforce our prediction that, by 2025, the China-India economic relationship is likely to be among the ten most important bilateral relationships in the world.

Table 1.5   China-India: The World's Fastest-Growing Trade Relationship

Trading Partner	China's Bilateral Trade (US$billions)			India's Bilateral Trade (US$billions)		
	2000	2012	Growth Rate (%)	2000	2012	Growth Rate (%)
India	3	69	29.8%	–	–	–
China	–	–	–	3	69	29.8%
U.S.	74	486	17.0%	14	62	13.2%
E.U.	75	579	18.6%	27	123	13.5%
Japan	84	330	12.1%	4	19	13.9%
South Korea	39	257	17.0%	2	18	20.1%
Russia	8	88	22.1%	2	7	11.0%
Association of Southeast Asian Nations (ASEAN)	39	400	21.4%	10	78	18.7%
Latin America	12	259	29.2%	2	44	29.4%
West Asia	14	204	25.0%	9	190	28.9%
Africa	11	198	27.2%	8	69	19.7%
World	474	3967	19.4%	95	780	19.2%

Note: During 2000–2012, world trade grew at a compounded annual rate of 9.2 percent.

Source: UNCTAD; China India Institute analysis.

While the data on bilateral trade tell a story of growing economic ties, they hide an important substory: the growing imbalance in favor of China (see Figure 1.6). Although China's trade surplus with India is consistent with its trade surplus with other economies, such as those of the United States and Europe (and indeed, the rest of the world), that has not been much of a comfort to India. The lopsided trade has been a source of growing tension between the two countries.

However, if we place India's trade deficit in the context of its overall trade deficit with the world at large, it becomes clear that the primary challenge for India lies *not* in its trade relationship with China but in its rapidly growing worldwide import bill. Figure 1.7 provides data on (a) India's worldwide trade deficit and (b) the trade deficit with China as a ratio of the worldwide trade deficit.

As Figure 1.7(b) tells us, India's trade deficit with China has hovered at around a fifth of its total trade deficit for more than a decade. Clearly, other goods accounting for four-fifths of India's trade deficit are an even bigger challenge for the country. Table 1.6 sheds light on the composition of India's trade with China as well as worldwide.

From these data, it is abundantly clear that India's primary trade challenge arises from its dependence on imported fuels and its citizens' love of gold. The trade deficit with China is important but not the biggest challenge.

It is difficult for us to see a quick resolution of the trade tensions between the two countries. Government and corporate leaders in India routinely lament that the trade imbalance would somehow vanish if only China would remove barriers

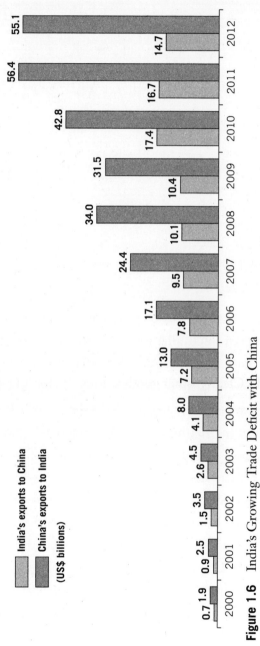

Figure 1.6 India's Growing Trade Deficit with China

Source: UNCTAD; China India Institute analysis.

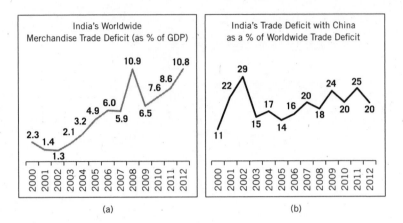

Figure 1.7 India's Trade Deficit with China in the Context of Its Worldwide Trade Deficit

Source: UNCTAD; China India Institute analysis.

to market access to Indian pharmaceuticals and IT services. As proponents of free trade, we agree that both governments should continue to press upon each other the need to start lowering and eventually removing many remaining barriers to international trade. At the same time, however, we believe that, given the differing nature of the two countries' comparative advantages, India would still continue to suffer from a trade deficit with China for several more years.

India is indeed a global power in generic pharmaceuticals and IT services. However, given the very low price of generic drugs, in 2012 India's global exports of pharmaceutical products added up to only US$11 billion. And given the brutal competition and extreme price sensitivity of the Chinese pharmaceutical market, we see the potential for Indian exports of such products to China as relatively limited. As for IT services, another sector

Table 1.6 India's Primary Trade Challenge: Large Dependence on Imported Energy Resources

Product Category	India's Merchandise Trade in 2012 (US$billions)					
	Worldwide			With China		
	Exports	Imports	Balance	Exports	Imports	Balance
Fuels	54	191	(137)	–	–	–
Nonmonetary gold	–	39	(39)	–	–	–
Pearls, precious stones, and the like	23	23	–	–	–	–
Other primary commodities	53	51	2	10[a]	–	10
Manufactured goods	157	176	(19)	5	48[b]	(43)
Miscellaneous other	3	9	(6)	–	6	(6)
TOTAL	280	489	(199)	15	54	(39)

[a]Mainly iron core, copper, cotton, and other commodities.
[b]Mainly capital goods such as power plant equipment, telecom equipment, and other types of electrical equipment. Also includes about US$8 billion in organic chemicals and fertilizers.
Source: UNCTAD; China India Institute analysis.

where India is a global leader, language differences are a natural barrier to Indian companies' ability to export such services to Chinese customers. This is precisely why the bulk of India's IT services are exported to English-speaking markets such as the United States, Canada, the United Kingdom, and Australia.

Other sectors where India is a significant exporter, such as automotive and textiles, also pose challenges. In both sectors, the scale of Chinese companies is much larger than that of their Indian peers. Thus it is hard to imagine how Indian companies could make much headway in either sector by attempting exports from India to China.

The long-term solution to India's unbalanced trade lies in reducing the country's dependence on imported fuels (by eliminating subsidies for consumers and aggressively promoting exploration and production within its borders), giving its citizens channels other than gold for investing their savings, and becoming a manufacturing power to rival China. On the last point, we believe that, in the short to medium term, Chinese exports to India should generally be welcomed rather than discouraged, as many of them are competitively priced capital goods.[19]

Chinese capital goods are often about 30 percent less expensive than imports from the United States, Europe, or Japan. They also come with low-cost financing from Chinese banks such as the Export Import Bank of China and China Development Bank.[20] As a result, Chinese capital goods unwittingly help accelerate the buildup of India's infrastructure and the eventual emergence of India as a manufacturing rival to China. India's policy makers might want to look at China's trade relationship with Japan, Germany, and South Korea. Despite the fact that China is extremely powerful in manufacturing, it continues to run a trade deficit with all three countries—a primary reason being that all three are major suppliers of top-end capital equipment to China.

DIRECT INVESTMENTS: THE NEW FRONTIER

Economic ties between China and India have begun to diversify beyond trade to include direct equity investments in R&D and manufacturing. At the end of 2012, the total stock of Chinese foreign direct investment (FDI) in India was about US$800 million. Conversely, the total stock of Indian FDI in China was about US$500 million.[21] These are still the early days of investment-based ties. We anticipate that, by 2020, the picture will look dramatically different.

To put the China-India numbers into context, the stock of Indian companies' FDI in China is less than 1 percent of their total FDI stock globally. For Chinese investments in India, the equivalent figure is about 0.2 percent. Notably, too, both China and India are still at an early stage in the game of creating global champions. At present, China's and India's worldwide shares of outbound FDI stock are 2.15 percent and 0.15 percent, respectively, a fraction of the numbers for the United States (22.0 percent), Japan (4.5 percent), or Germany (6.6 percent). Over the next ten years, as the global shares of the Chinese and Indian economies grow, these numbers are likely to grow significantly.

Prominent examples of Indian companies operating (not just trading) in China include companies in the information technology sector (Tata Consultancy Services, Infosys, and NIIT) as well as manufacturing (Birla Group, Mahindra Tractors, Thermax, and the nuts and bolts business of Sundaram Fasteners). In addition, as we noted earlier, Tata Motors'

Jaguar Land Rover subsidiary is currently erecting a large manufacturing and R&D base in China. These facilities, being set up through a joint venture with Chery Automobile, are scheduled to become operational in 2014.

Prominent examples of Chinese companies with investments in India include Huawei (telecommunications equipment), Lenovo (personal computers), Haier (home appliances), Shanghai Auto (cars), and Sany (construction machinery). Examples of other Chinese companies contemplating investment in India include CNR and CSR (railway locomotives), Great Wall Motor (cars), and Wanfeng (aluminum wheels for the automotive sector).

Given India's current weakness in manufacturing, is there any reason to believe that Indian companies can enter China via investments and succeed? We believe that the answer is "yes" for the following reasons:

• Many of the larger Indian companies are world class in terms of their leadership and organizational capabilities. If they decide to play in China by manufacturing in China (or, in the case of the services sector, by producing the services in China), they are no longer constrained by India's weakness in infrastructure. Organizational capabilities are highly fungible across borders. True, China poses many challenges for all multinationals (as we discuss in Chapter Two). However, in many industries, given time and commitment, companies can learn to overcome many of these challenges. It is also important to remember that the new leadership in China appears committed to opening up larger sections of the economy to entry by foreign players.

• The odds of success go up significantly if Indian companies design their China strategies with a global mindset. In most cases, it would be counterproductive to think in terms of "how to compete with Chinese companies for Chinese customers in China." Instead, the more relevant questions should be: "How can we leverage our global (including Indian) capabilities and relationships to win in China? How can we leverage our Chinese presence to become a stronger competitor in India, the rest of Asia, and worldwide? Could we partner with a Chinese company to take on Chinese and other multinational companies not just in China but also globally?"

• In many cases, the road from India to China (and similarly from China to India) may run not across the Himalayas but via a third country such as Singapore, South Korea, Japan, the United States, the United Kingdom, Germany, or France. Take Tata Motors and Jaguar Land Rover. Globally, Indian car companies are not known as either brand or technology leaders. Thus any attempt by Tata Motors to crack the Chinese market via direct entry would have been enormously risky. However, by acquiring JLR, Tata Motors has been able to leverage the brand and technical strengths of JLR to become hugely successful in China. With the rapid growth of cross-border acquisitions by both Chinese and Indian companies, we anticipate that the indirect route will become increasingly common as a way for Indian and Chinese companies to enter each other's markets. This is precisely how Lenovo entered

India in 2005 after acquiring IBM's PC business. As other examples, look at Mahindra Group's acquisition of the Korean company SsangYong and its plans to leverage this base to enter the Chinese market for SUVs, the Chinese company Geely's acquisition of Volvo Cars and the relative ease with which it could now enter the Indian car market, or Sany's acquisition of the German pump maker Putzmeister and its plans to leverage the acquired company's brand name and technologies globally. This process has just begun.

There are also interesting new developments under way with regard to Chinese investments in India. As signaled by Premier Li Keqiang's decision to visit India on his maiden official trip, Chinese leaders accept the inevitability of India's rise as one of the four or five largest economies by 2025. They have also publicly accepted the nonsustainability of trade ties that remain hugely unbalanced in China's favor. As a result, China's leaders are also extremely keen to transform the economic ties between the two nations to include not just trade but also investments. At the time of this writing, a high-powered Chinese delegation comprising government as well as corporate leaders from a number of sectors (banking, water, power, tourism, and agriculture) was visiting India to meet with senior officials in the states of Haryana and Uttar Pradesh. Their mission: discuss opportunities to set up industrial parks in these states. China has large reserves of capital as well as enormous experience in setting up well-functioning industrial parks. A collaboration in this area, perhaps through a joint venture with an Indian partner, has the potential to be a major win for both sides.[22]

To paraphrase Amazon CEO Jeff Bezos' oft-repeated observation about his company, this is still "day one" in the evolution of economic ties between India and China. The opportunities are large, but so are the challenges. In an increasingly competitive global environment, there are no easy or quick wins. Indian and Chinese companies that emerge as global winners by 2025 will be those that commit to the other country for the long haul. Corporate leaders who decide to play this game will need to be *shrewd*, so as not to lose their shirts; *creative*, in order to overcome initial handicaps; and *global thinkers*, in order to compete effectively with local players.

2

Succeeding in China
Opportunities and Challenges

There is near consensus that China's economy has entered a new phase. The era of double-digit economic growth is over. The IMF projects that the country's economy will grow by 7.6 percent in 2013 and 7.3 percent in 2014. During the following ten to fifteen years, the growth rate is more likely to average around 6 percent.[1]

For an economy of China's size and current stage of economic development, a 5- to 6-percent sustained growth rate would still be very robust. By all accounts, China is on course to overtake the United States and become the world's largest economy by 2025. This means that, for the foreseeable future, China will remain one of the most attractive markets for the world's multinational corporations (MNCs), including Indian MNCs. In this chapter, we highlight the benefits of being in China, the industry sectors that offer particularly high growth opportunities in China, and the challenges that Indian MNCs eyeing China must be aware of so that they can plan ahead and put in place de-risking strategies.

CHINA OPPORTUNITIES

We begin by arguing that Indian companies should think of the value proposition for operating in China from a broader "in China for the world" lens rather than a narrower "in China for China" lens. We then present an overview of those sectors of the Chinese economy that are likely to grow even faster than the economy as a whole.

Can Indian companies succeed in China? The answer depends not just on whether a particular Indian company has advantages that would enable it to succeed in China but also on the strategies that it may devise to overcome any India-specific disadvantages. As we discuss later in the book, Tata Motors would have found it extremely difficult to enter and succeed in China's auto sector by going directly from India to China. Yet by taking an indirect route—from India to the United Kingdom to China—through the acquisition of Jaguar Land Rover, Tata Motors is doing extremely well in China. The indirect route enabled Tata Motors to combine the company's organizational and post-merger integration skills with the technological and brand strengths of JLR to crack open the Chinese market for luxury cars. Such an indirect route could be a viable and attractive strategy for many Indian companies across a wide array of industries.

In China for China *and the World*

In assessing the value proposition from China, Indian executives should think broadly rather than narrowly—that is, not just in terms of how one can grow and earn in China but also in terms of how operating in China could make the company stronger—within India, regionally in other countries outside China, and globally. To illustrate, consider the B2B sector. A number of foreign multinationals (such as Caterpillar, John Deere, ABB, Schneider Electric, and others) are major customers of Indian companies in India. If the Indian company is not present in China, it runs the risk that it could be displaced by its Chinese counterpart if the latter decides to set up operations in India. On the other hand, by operating in both India and China, the Indian company could enjoy the benefits of bigger scale, a stronger relationship with the customer, and tougher entry barriers for its Chinese competitors. This is precisely the strategy followed by Sundaram Fasteners, which has become a key supplier to western heavy machinery manufacturers in India and China as well as the rest of the world.

In the information technology sector, Japan and South Korea are important markets that Indian companies have great difficulty cracking, largely because of language differences. This disadvantage can be easily overcome by serving these markets from delivery centers in northeastern China, where many people are fluent in one or both of these languages—a strategy that TCS (Tata Consultancy Services), Infosys, and a few other IT companies have adopted successfully. In manufacturing-intensive industries, an Indian company could leverage China's excellent infrastructure and the lower cost of many inputs to use it as an export base. Mahindra Group is doing this in tractors by exporting to the United States from both India and China.

It may also be possible to leverage a presence in the Chinese market to learn new business models and accelerate the company's pace of innovation. Upon its entry into China, NIIT learned that it could expand far more rapidly by partnering with universities, which would license NIIT's curriculum and instructional methodologies and have these replace their own curriculum. This "NIIT Inside" approach is very different from what the company had followed in India. Having designed and implemented this approach successfully in China, NIIT finds that this has opened up new opportunities for the company in other markets as well.

It is also worth keeping in mind that, as Indian and Chinese companies expand their wings globally, there may be opportunities for them to collaborate in third countries. The partnership between Bharti Airtel and Huawei Technologies in Africa is a case in point. Airtel is the second-largest mobile operator in Africa, and Huawei has emerged as one of its key network technology partners on the continent. In terms of organizational skills, IT capabilities, and English language fluency, Indian companies are much stronger than Chinese companies of equivalent size. On the other hand, Chinese companies often have a lower cost of hardware and bring low-cost project financing and stronger project execution skills. Opportunities to leverage the two sides' complementary capabilities are more likely to emerge if the Indian company is present in China, is comfortable partnering with Chinese companies, and has built a base of valuable knowledge and relationships.

We now present an overview of some of the high-growth opportunities within China. To begin with, an important caveat is in order. As the world's second-largest economy, with a fifth of the world's population, China is not a niche economy. Even at a 5- to 6-percent annual growth rate in GDP, almost every industry—be it clothing, computers, or cars—is likely to be large and will keep growing. However, the nature of high-growth opportunities in China over the next five to ten years will be quite different from that in the recent past. Economic growth over the last ten years was led primarily by investments in infrastructure and real estate and feeder industries such as steel, cement, and construction equipment. This is no longer viable and these will remain slow-growth industries for many years. The bulk of the economic growth over the coming decade will be driven by a different set of industries—those that either tap into the challenges that China faces today or feed the growing shift toward consumption rather than investment.

B2B and B2C Services

Services currently account for about 43 percent of China's GDP—compared with 49 percent in the case of Malaysia, 58 percent for South Korea, 73 percent for Japan, and 79 percent for the United States. It is a certainty that, as China becomes more affluent, the services sector will grow notably faster than GDP. This growth should be equally large in the case of both B2B as well as B2C services.

Consider B2B services first. With the growth of the Chinese economy, Chinese companies have also become much bigger and increasingly global. Look at the developments since 2005. That year, there were sixteen companies from China in the *Fortune Global 500* list, which includes the five hundred largest publicly listed companies in the world by revenue. Of these, the largest—Sinopec—had revenues of US$75 billion. The 2013 list included 89 companies from China. Sinopec was still the largest Chinese company; however, its revenues had grown by more than five times, to US$428 billion. On the globalization front, by the end of 2005, the stock of outbound foreign direct investment by Chinese companies was US$57 billion. At the end of 2012, it was nine times as large—US$509 billion.[2] As a direct corollary of growing size and global expansion, there has also been an increase in the number of Chinese companies that are now publicly listed. In 2000, there were only 572 companies listed on the Shanghai Stock Exchange. By 2005, this number had grown to 834, and by 2011, to 931. All of these trends are creating an explosive growth in the demand for professional services of all types—accounting, legal, information technology, management consulting, marketing and advertising, public relations, and so forth.

In the B2C sector, high-growth opportunities exist in almost all domains—child care, elder care, health care, and financial services. Take child care. According to the 2010 census, 74 percent of working age Chinese women work outside the home. However, for urban women, the figure drops to 61 percent. A major factor behind the difference is the need to look after the child. In rural areas, parents can pitch in to help with child care. However, this is much more difficult for urban couples, as apartments are very small. Also, given China's restrictive *hukou* system (the equivalent of an internal visa), parents may have difficulty getting residency permits for the city. Thus professional child care is fast becoming a high-growth industry. A similar but different situation applies to elder care. The urban couple may be the only children of their parents, yet the parents live in the countryside, and the young couple is unable to look after them in their old age. This creates a growing market for professional elder care.

Health care and financial services are large and rapidly growing service industries in China. As the population becomes older but also more affluent, it is clear that the health care industry will grow much faster than GDP. Similarly, given rising affluence, Chinese adults have a growing pool of savings. At present, the bulk of the savings are kept in bank accounts (where they earn extremely low interest rates set by the government) or invested in real estate. The new leadership has signaled that it will start to liberalize the banking sector and may also start allowing people to invest their savings in foreign equities and bonds. As these policies are implemented, the financial services being offered become more diverse, and participation in financial markets becomes more widespread, the financial services industry will grow extremely rapidly.

Industrial Automation

As a result of its one-child policy, China has become a rapidly aging society and is now beginning to face labor shortages. Consider two key facts:

- In 2000, the median age in China was 29.6 years. It increased to 34.6 years by 2010 and is expected to increase further to 39.6 years by 2025. In contrast, the median age of the Indian population is several years younger and the age gap between the two countries is growing. In 2000, India's median age was 23.0 years (6.6 years less than China's). By 2010, India's median age increased to 25.5 years (9.1 years younger than China's). By 2025, India's median age is expected to be 29.9 years (fully 9.7 years younger than China's).[3]

- From 2000 to 2010, the size of China's labor force (people in the fifteen-to-sixty-four age range) grew from 853 million to 983 million; that is, at a rate of 1.4 percent a year. Since 2010, however, the growth rate has slowed to only 0.4 percent a year. From 2015 onward, China's labor pool is predicted to start shrinking at the rate of 0.5 percent a year.[4]

As a result of rising incomes, aging population, and slower growth of the labor pool, wages in China have been increasing much faster than inflation. According to government data, during 2008–2013 manufacturing wages went up at an annual rate of 15 percent in yuan terms and 18 percent in U.S. dollars. Estimated manufacturing wages in January 2013 were US$2.92 per hour.[5]

These trends have made industrial companies, especially those on the east coast, extremely eager to shift from manual labor to automation—a trend that is being encouraged by the government, which is keen to have the east coast focus on high-technology manufacturing, knowledge-intensive industries, and the services sector. As an indicator of the ongoing trends, look at Foxconn, the Taiwanese company that assembles electronics hardware for almost all of the world's major corporations, including Apple. As of 2011, Foxconn employed about 1.2 million workers in China. Because of rising wages as well as the fact that young Chinese workers are no longer keen to do tedious manual work, CEO Terry Gou announced that the company would start installing robots in its factories, eventually reaching as many as one million robots.[6]

The growing imperative for industrial automation offers opportunities to a host of companies, including industrial machinery manufacturers, instrumentation suppliers, engineering services companies, software developers, and the providers of other complementary components and services.

Enhancing Energy Efficiency

China's economy is far more energy-intensive relative to other large economies. In 2012, China's share of world GDP was a little less than 12 percent. However, it consumed 22 percent of the world's total energy—partly because of its large population (about 20 percent of the world) and partly because heavier industries such as steel and cement consume far more energy than lighter industries or the services sector.

China also happens to be one of the world's largest energy producers. However, the country faces two major challenges. First, it consumes more energy than it produces and the country's reliance on imported energy is growing. In 2000, China enjoyed near parity in domestic energy needs and production. By 2012, however, China was importing about 8 percent of its total energy needs. China's dependence on imported oil is even greater—about 57 percent of its total consumption in 2012. Second, China relies far too heavily on coal. Although China has an abundance of coal deposits, pollution has now become an extremely serious concern. Both of these challenges mean that, along with pollution control, energy efficiency is one of the government's most important economic goals. The twelfth five-year plan targeted a 16-percent reduction in the GDP's energy intensity during 2011–2015. We anticipate that the energy efficiency targets for the thirteenth five-year plan covering 2016–2020 could be even more ambitious.

These national challenges and policy goals present huge opportunities to companies that can help China at any point in the energy value chain—energy exploration, energy production, energy distribution, and more efficient energy consumption. Although the government may reserve some of these opportunities for domestic state-owned enterprises (SOEs), many of these are and will remain open to any foreign company that can offer relevant solutions. These opportunities are vast and cut across almost all industrial sectors—for example, better technologies for the production of renewable energy, auto components and tires that increase the energy efficiency of cars, components for home appliances that cut energy consumption, control systems that reduce energy consumption in factories and buildings, and so forth.

Combating Pollution Control

Despite growing reliance on nonfossil sources of energy (solar, wind, hydro and nuclear energy), coal is still the raw material for over 75 percent of electricity production in China. Over the last thirty years, breakneck industrial development has meant a rapidly rising demand for electricity and thus a massive increase in the use of coal to generate the needed electricity. The health implications of this dependence on coal have now started to become clear.

Chinese cities suffer from much worse air pollution than those in almost any other country in the world. In January 2013, PM2.5[7] readings in Beijing exceeded 1000 on many days, forty times the WHO standard for clean air.[8] High levels of air pollution are a serious problem in almost all major Chinese cities. For several days in October 2013, very high levels of smog and extremely low visibility forced the authorities in the northeastern city of Harbin to close the airport and many roads to prevent accidents. Citizens as well as government officials are becoming increasingly alarmed at the prospect of chronic lung problems and premature deaths. A recent article in *China Daily*, the premier English-language newspaper, reported the government's growing seriousness about combating air pollution:

> An inspection campaign on how *air pollution* is being controlled will be launched in key areas of China, the Ministry

of Environmental Protection has announced . . . The inspection team will check on how local governments are enforcing the Airborne Pollution Prevention and Control Action Plan, which is aimed at reducing air pollution with stricter limits on the levels of PM2.5, airborne particles measuring less than 2.5 microns in diameter.

The inspection will focus on the operation of desulfurization, denitrification and dedusting facilities at enterprises, pollutant emissions and the replacement of coal-fired boilers. Small companies violating air pollution control regulations will be shut down. Departments and officials found to be breaking the law will be held responsible. Media organizations are invited to participate in the inspection.[9]

Water pollution, caused by industrial effluents, has also become a serious challenge in China. The new administration's commitment to these challenges means that companies which provide technologies, equipment, and solutions to prevent and help redress all types of pollution should find large and growing opportunities in the country.

Agricultural Productivity and Water Scarcity

China's land area is three times that of India. However, a far greater chunk of China's land consists of deserts and mountains than is the case for India. According to World Bank estimates, only one-eighth of China's land area is arable; for India, the comparable figure is over half of all land area. This means that, even though China has a bigger population, its *arable* land is only about two-thirds the size of India's. Further, as in India, the size of the average Chinese farm is very small.

Two other factors add to the challenge of food security in China. First, China suffers from an acute scarcity of fresh water. In China, renewable fresh water resources on a per capita basis are only about one-third of the world average (compared with an even worse one-sixth of the world average in India). Second, with growing per capita incomes, Chinese eating habits have changed dramatically over the last thirty years. The average Chinese citizen eats far more meat today than was the case for the earlier generation. Getting one's calories from meat requires far larger quantities of grain compared with getting them from bread, buns, or rice. Getting the same calories from beef requires about five to seven times as much grain, and from pork or chicken, about two to three times as much grain as getting them directly from the grain.

Not surprisingly, China's imports of almost all types of grains (corn, wheat, and rice) as well as meats are rising. Given the criticality of food security, the government regards such a trend as unacceptable and seems determined to boost agricultural productivity and water conservation dramatically over the next ten years. The initial moves in the government's plans are already under way—accelerating the consolidation of farms by letting farmers sell their rights to till an allotted plot of land.

The government's push to boost agricultural productivity offers opportunities to any company that can play an enabling role. Illustrative examples of some industries that should grow at a faster rate than GDP include farm machinery (for example, larger and more powerful tractors) and seed technologies (for example, genetically modified seeds that require less water and are genetically more resistant to insects or other sources of crop damage). The government is equally determined to find ways to ensure water conservation and, to the extent possible, expansion of fresh water resources. These national imperatives should offer high-growth opportunities to companies that bring technologies, equipment, and solutions in areas such as drip irrigation, water filtration, sea water desalination, rainwater conservation, and recycling of used water.

Luxury Goods and Tourism

Growing affluence means that most Chinese citizens are now able to meet their basic needs and thus are no longer first-time buyers of daily necessities such as toothpaste, laundry detergents, chocolate, TVs, or home appliances. In urban China, a growing number of households are also graduating from buying their first car to buying the second one. As consumers evolve from being first-time buyers to becoming repeat buyers, they are trading up. They want to buy not just basic toothpaste but teeth-whitening toothpaste, not just basic laundry detergent but one that also contains fabric softener.

As the entire bell curve of population frequency versus per capita income moves to the right, the proportion of the population that is desperately poor is falling rapidly and the upper income (by global standards) proportion is rising sharply. As a result, the demand for luxury goods is rising at a much faster pace than the overall growth in GDP or retail sales. During 2007–2012, the sales of luxury brands in China grew at a compounded annual rate of over 30 percent, compared with an 8-percent growth rate in the worldwide sales of these goods. Mainland Chinese customers now account for about 20 percent of worldwide luxury goods sales—half through retail stores in China and half on shopping trips to foreign countries. And consider the data on luxury cars. During the first half of 2013, China's GDP grew by about 7.5 percent. In contrast, the sales of passenger cars grew by 13.8 percent—and the sales of luxury cars grew even faster. In the first half of 2013, the top three German luxury brands (Audi, BMW, and Mercedes-Benz) reported combined sales that were about 15 percent greater than during the same period in 2012. The Tata Motors subsidiary Jaguar Land Rover has been a direct beneficiary of this rapid growth in demand for luxury cars.

Aside from buying luxury goods, Chinese consumers are also travelling in ever-larger numbers, domestically as well as abroad. The amount of money spent by Chinese on domestic tourism grew by over six times from 2000 to 2011. International tourism grew even faster. The number of outbound travelers from China was seven times as large in 2011 as in 2000. During this period there has also been a significant increase in the amount of money spent by each traveler. In terms of total value, Chinese tourists are now the world's largest spenders on international tourism, having overtaken the Germans and the Americans in 2012. Greater travel and tourism is creating a growing demand for all types of goods and services that form part of this phenomenon—airline travel, hotels, restaurants, personal shopping, and gifts and souvenirs.

CHINA CHALLENGES

It was not easy for the CEO of a large Indian auto component company to face its board of directors in the summer of 2013 and announce a write-down of nearly 30 percent of its investment in China. While pacing the floor before the board meeting, he ruminated on how rosy the opportunity had looked when they decided four years earlier to sign a joint venture (JV) agreement for this investment. He remembered the ribbon-cutting ceremonies and lavish banquets that followed. The mayor and his underlings had made encouraging speeches welcoming Indian investments and promising all help. True to the mayor's word, the local authorities and JV partners delivered on their promise, and the project execution was far better than their experience had been in India.

The auto market in China was expected to continue booming for a decade and become bigger than the U.S. auto market (then the largest in the world). Even if one made pessimistic assumptions, the project looked to be a no-brainer. From every angle, it looked to be a great strategic investment and a key element of the company's globalization plans. Many of the company's global auto customers were moving to China. An attractive opportunity to tie up a majority-owned JV with a well-known state-owned enterprise (SOE) was too good to pass up. Establishing a new plant from scratch was easy, and the infrastructure was much better than in India. The factory was off to a good start.

What followed were a few years of expansion with declining margins and many bouts of cultural clashes within the JV management as well as the board. The SOE was more interested in expanding for the future, with ambitious plans for capital expenditure that would create employment and increase the top line—but crater the bottom line, at least in the medium term. Months of discussions finally brought matters to a breaking point. It was clear that they had not understood the culture of the JV partner and had underestimated the challenge of managing the JV. It was, as the Chinese saying goes, "same bed, different dreams."

As this case illustrates, it is important for leaders of any Indian (indeed, any foreign) company to have a good understanding of the landscape they are likely to encounter when they start planning to enter China. The terrain is likely to be bumpy, with unexpected challenges that may crop up at any time. However, as Indian executives and entrepreneurs know only too well, this is no different from operating in India, which has its own share of unique obstacle courses that businessmen and women need to overcome. In some ways, the scale of India and the uncertainties inherent in such a developing country environment may make Indian companies even better prepared to handle these in China. We next discuss the challenges that are peculiar to China. These fall into two major categories: (1) cultural and political challenges and (2) economic challenges.

Cultural and Political Challenges

We begin with an analysis of the cultural and political challenges that Indian companies are likely to face in China. Although many of these challenges are faced by multinationals from

61

other countries as well, some are unique to companies from India—such as the difficulty of separating the economic from the political relationship between the two nations.

Indian Mindset vis-à-vis China

For Indian executives, one of the biggest obstacles to doing business in China is, ironically, the current Indian mindset. Politics trumps economics for many in India. We are not suggesting that Indians should forget the boundary or other disputes with China. The trust deficit will start vanishing only when these issues appear close to resolution. We do argue, however, that there is no reason why geopolitical disagreements with China should stand in the way of a robust economic relationship between the two countries.

Look at the relationship between China and Japan. Japan attacked and occupied Chinese territory for decades. In the six-week-long Nanjing Massacre in 1937, the Japanese Imperial Army is believed to have killed tens of thousands (some estimates put the number at over 250,000) of unarmed civilians and soldiers. Chinese citizens remain bitter about this episode. In fact, millions of Chinese citizens continue to hate the Japanese. China and Japan also have a border disagreement over who owns certain islands in the East China Sea. In terms of the risk of a military conflict, this disagreement is far more serious than the boundary disputes between India and China. Despite these tensions, Chinese and Japanese companies continue to do robust business with each other. In 2012, the bilateral trade between China and Japan was a whopping US$330 billion with

China importing more from Japan than exporting to it. Many Japanese companies (such as Toyota, Nissan, Honda, Hitachi, and many others) are extremely successful in China. In turn, Chinese companies (such as Lenovo and Haier) have started to make acquisitions in Japan.

The China-Japan relationship holds important lessons for business leaders in India. Indian business leaders who wish to succeed in China need to compartmentalize and separate their commercial ties from the two countries' geopolitical relationship. This would be no different from the approach that both Indian and Chinese political leaders have been following for the past decade. The Chinese are a very pragmatic people and, despite being ruled by the Communist Party, are at least as business-minded as the Americans, if not more so. Further, there's a better than even chance that stronger economic linkages will make it easier for the political leaders on both sides to find a peaceful and mutually acceptable resolution to the boundary issues.

Differing Values—But Not Entirely

There are indeed some important differences in the value systems of the Indians and the Chinese. However, because the Chinese look different from Indians, speak a very different language, and eat very different food, it is easy for Indians to assume that the Chinese are difficult to gauge and do business with—almost as if they live on a different planet. In fact, many seasoned businesspeople would say that, in terms of value systems, the Chinese and Japanese probably differ more from each other than the Chinese and the Indians—even though the Chinese and Japanese have similar facial features and there is more common ground in their foods than there is in Chinese and Indian foods. Appearances often can be deceptive!

We begin with some of the major commonalities between the Indian and Chinese cultures. Living in two of the world's oldest civilizations, both peoples are extremely proud of their heritage, have an abiding sense of their history, know that theirs were once among the richest and most advanced societies, and believe that it is their destiny to once again take a leadership position in the world. Thus neither side is willing to be pushed around. Disagreements must be handled tactfully, as it is important to preserve the other side's dignity ("face"). Like Indians, the Chinese also treat others so as to save the other's face. When asked to do the impossible, it's rare for them to bluntly say "No, I cannot do it"; instead, they are more likely to respond with "I'll try my best." Coming from old civilizations with a long history of trading, Indians and Chinese are also highly skilled negotiators, and their cultures have bred entrepreneurs who have excelled globally. The success of the Chinese and Indian diaspora is living proof of this similarity in traits.

Both cultures are also virtually identical in terms of the extremely high importance given to respect for the elderly and ancestor worship—due most likely to similarities in religious traditions between Hinduism and Buddhism. In fact, even some of the superstitions are similar. In addition, both focus on the family, children, education, math and science, and saving for the future. This could be one of the major reasons why the list of top performers in many of the best schools and colleges in the United States tends to include a disproportionate number of Indian and Chinese students and why immigrants from the two countries have been founders or cofounders of more than a third of all technology startups in Silicon Valley. Surprising as it may sound to Indians, the Chinese are just as individualistic as they are. Almost twenty years ago, a Japanese anthropologist made an insightful remark to one of the authors: "Isn't it interesting that in China you have capitalists living under a communist system, whereas in Japan you have communists living in a capitalist system?" Both societies are also very relationship-oriented, although, given the far greater dominance of the government in China, relationships (or *guanxi*) are even more important in China than in India. *Guanxi* in business terms often translates to "Let us be friends first and then become business partners." Loyalty is a highly regarded trait in both societies.

The differences in the two societies' value systems are as sharp and important as the commonalities. Perhaps the most important difference is that the Chinese are far more pragmatic and action-oriented than the Indians. As the Nobel Laureate Amartya Sen observed, Indians *love* to argue.[10] The typical Chinese tends to be much more action oriented. Reflecting their Confucian traditions as well as more than half a century of communist rule, the Chinese are also much more hierarchical and respectful of authority than the Indians. It is not easy to get Chinese employees to challenge their leaders' ideas. Contrast this with India, where, if you are placed in a room with young professionals, you may have a tough time saying much, as everyone is likely to have an idea and will want to beat the others to expressing it first. Given their respect for authority, the Chinese are also far more disciplined than the Indians. Many western executives with experience in both countries have commented to us that they find their Indian staff to be more creative but the Chinese staff to be better at execution. Reflecting their greater discipline, the Chinese are also very punctual. The Indian concepts of *chalta hai* ("anything goes") or "Indian stretchable time" would come across as quite strange to many Chinese counterparts. While the Indian tradition encourages debate, ideation, and creativity, the Chinese orderliness and discipline can make Chinese staff a formidable execution machine. To many in senior management, a combination of the two would be a dream team.

The vast differences in the two societies' languages and eating habits often pose a challenge for many Indian executives, especially if they are visiting China for the first time. We should add that, on both dimensions, the situation is fast improving. The Chinese government requires all children to start learning English right from elementary school. Thus most urban professionals up to about age forty tend to be passably good in English. In fact, recent college graduates are often very fluent in English. In any case, it is always wiser for even Mandarin-speaking foreigners to use the services of an excellent translator (hired by them, not the other party) when discussing business issues with Chinese counterparts. Otherwise, one runs the risk of missing subtleties, which in an ancient language like Mandarin are many. It goes without saying that any Indian executive assigned to work in China for an extended period must invest time and effort up front to become moderately fluent in spoken Mandarin. This is actually far easier than one might imagine. Spoken Mandarin has a simpler and cleaner grammatical structure than English. Being able to communicate even moderately in Chinese will make social interactions much easier and a whole lot more enjoyable.

With respect to food, note that meals are an important part of business dealings. Getting to know each other over long multicourse dinners is often an important starting point for successful business deals. For vegetarian Indians, Chinese cuisine can present challenges. Chinese do eat plenty of fruits and vegetables. However, they are ardent meat lovers. Also, their interpretation of vegetarian food may differ from that of most Indians, as they may assume that eggs (or even fish) are really vegetarian food. On the plus side, most Chinese restaurants do prepare purely vegetarian dishes. Also, western fast-food chains such as Pizza Hut and McDonald's are becoming ubiquitous even in smaller towns. Thus a visiting Indian executive can almost always find familiar food. As well, Indian restaurants have begun to crop up in many Chinese cities.

The Omnipresent Government

The Chinese government remains the dominant provider and regulator and acts as a very visible and key player commercially. It is almost as if the government was simultaneously "Brahma, Vishnu, and Mahesh"—the three main faces of the Hindu god as creator, regulator, and destroyer! Through its broad regulatory powers and ownership of enterprises in most sectors belonging to the "commanding heights" of the economy (banking, insurance, telecom operations, airlines, steel, aluminum, cement, rail equipment, aircraft, and so on), the Chinese government is often both a regulator and a customer, thereby playing a bigger role than is true for any other large economy.

Prior to the start of the Deng Xiaoping reforms in 1978, there was no concept of private property whatsoever. The government owned everything ("even the chicken in your backyard," as a senior officer in the government said to us). With the launch of the reforms, the concept of private property began to be established and the state started to make room for the market. This development picked up steam in the 1990s with the privatization of hundreds of state-owned enterprises. In 2001, China joined the WTO and relaxed many of the barriers to foreign companies. Since 2002, however, the role of state-owned enterprises has resurged. During 2002–2012, the government focused almost single-mindedly on building infrastructure. Because most of the companies involved in implementing this mission were state-owned, they were the ones that cornered the bulk of the loans from major banks, almost all of which are also state-owned. As a result, over the last ten years the private sector has found itself starved of capital, and with some exceptions—such as the well-known internet companies—has not been able to grow at the same pace as the SOEs. A senior central government minister once compared the Chinese economy to a bird cage in which private companies are the birds—caged by both explicit regulations and implicit expectations, with just enough freedom to move around but not enough to do as they please. All indications are that Premier Li Keqiang, the new economic czar, seems determined to start expanding the role of the market once again.

In the Chinese political system, there is no concept of separation of powers between the state (that is, the government) and the party. The Communist Party is the dominant power. While the government focuses on the economy, services to citizens, and economic development, the party focuses on setting policy, overseeing implementation, social stability, and internal security. Foreign executives may deal with government officers but must remember that key decisions will be finalized only after consultation with party representatives. Unlike in India, Chinese bureaucrats do not have independent constitutional powers. At senior levels, it is common for an individual to move often between the Communist Party, the government bureaucracy, and state-owned enterprises. For example, on more than one occasion, the executive chairman of Shanghai Auto (a state-owned enterprise) was simultaneously the CEO of the company as well as a member of the Shanghai Municipal People's Government. Similarly, provincial governors and city mayors are appointed, not elected. As a rule, they have to be trusted senior members of the Communist Party.

Despite the overall framework that the government is omnipresent, it would be wrong to think of the Chinese government as monolithic. Given China's size (geographic, population, and economic), the centuries-old Chinese saying "The mountains are high and the emperor is far away" still holds true. Political and economic power is distributed across various ministries, between the central, provincial, and local levels, and between the bureaucrats and the top echelons of state-owned enterprises. The various players do not always agree, even if they may pretend that they do. The implication for companies, both domestic and foreign, is that one needs to keep track of policies and regulations at all levels. Getting clearance at one level does not guarantee that you will not run afoul of regulations at another level. It's important to get agreements signed in writing, as overly enthusiastic bureaucrats may exceed their authority and later backtrack and resort to mediation or even litigation. Sometimes the political goals of the government may clash with that of the firm as, for example, in the widely watched case of the arrest of senior executives of Rio Tinto, the global mining giant. An espionage charge for "stealing state secrets" (in a context in which it is not always clear what is or is not a state secret) can create problems if relationships with various arms of the government are not managed properly.

Since the launch of the reforms in 1978, the overarching goal of the country's leaders has been to create an economically strong China. In pursuit of this goal, the leaders have used GDP growth as a clean, directly measurable, and most important measure of economic strength. As part of the five-year planning process, all provincial governors and city mayors are given targets for GDP growth and, as in a brutally demanding corporation (think of GE under "neutron Jack" Welch), are held accountable for delivering on these goals. The average tenure of a governor or mayor is about three years. Those who beat the targets are likely to get rewarded with a promotion or move to a more important province or city. Those who fail may find themselves demoted to much less desirable locations. This tough corporate-style management-by-objectives system for running the country has made local officials extremely hungry for investments that will bring technology and create jobs and economic growth quickly. If a foreign company—whether from India or anywhere else in the world—can help the local leaders achieve their assigned goals, chances are high that they will bend over backward to make life easy for the company. Of course, if the local mayor, governor, and/or party secretary gets transferred to another location, then it becomes imperative for the company to build *guanxi* (that is, good relationships) with the incoming leaders all over again.

The concentration of power also has a serious downside. According to many reports (such as those by Transparency International[11]), China—like India and almost every emerging economy—suffers from serious corruption. On more than one occasion, the very top leaders in China have publicly identified combating corruption as the single biggest challenge for the Communist Party and the country. The new leadership of President Xi Jinping and his colleagues appears to have become particularly aggressive in cracking down on corruption. For foreign companies and their executives, it has now become even more dangerous to engage in bribery or other types of unethical conduct. They may find themselves running afoul of not only the laws of their home country but also those of China.

Different Legal System

The decade-long Cultural Revolution in China wiped out almost all semblance of any legal system. Colleges were shut down, and the elite were sent to the countryside. Thus when Deng Xiaoping started the opening up process, he faced a herculean challenge with regard to setting up a legal system—a legal vacuum with no law schools, no lawyers, no trained judges, and no formal courts. The process was jump started by appointing trusted party leaders and military officers as judges. Over the last three decades, the legal system has become considerably more well-defined, with formal statutes, law schools, law firms, judges, and so forth.

However, there remain some important differences between the legal system in China and that in India or other countries rooted in Western traditions. First, legal codes are still being formed. Thus in many contexts it remains unclear what exactly is legal and what is not. This leaves a lot of room for interpretation by various authorities, including the judges. Second, because of the lack of separation of powers, judges will often take into account not only the statutes and the evidence but also their own personal judgment regarding what would be good for China. Third, at a more behavioral level, Chinese entrepreneurs and business executives have a reputation for treating a contract not as something that is binding but as more like an agreement whose validity depends only on what was known at the time of signing the contract.

These differences create serious challenges (and potential risks) for foreign companies. The typical approach adopted by experienced multinationals, whenever possible, is to insist on binding arbitration outside China (most often in Hong Kong or Singapore), thereby sidestepping the need to take a case to a Chinese court. Of course, this may not always be advisable or even possible; for example, when dealing with a unit of the Chinese government.

It is important not to underestimate the scale of the legal challenge, especially in the early phase of setting up a unit in China, when everything sounds pretty confusing and innumerable local well-wishers may offer their services to navigate and lubricate the complex system. The place to start is to set up a cross-functional accounting, HR, and legal team right at the inception stage. Corporate law, taxation, labor laws, employment code, visas and work permits, foreign exchange, banking rules, and accounting standards need to be examined to see what is applicable and relevant to a specific firm. This is exactly what TCS did when setting up its first entity in China in 2002. The company's Compliance Manual was so thorough that it received recognition from the local city authorities—as well as a medal!

Economic Challenges

We now discuss the economic challenges that a multinational company planning to enter China may encounter. Awareness of these challenges can play an important role in helping the company design a more robust strategy for operating and competing in China.

Vast and Diverse

China is a large country by almost every measure that matters—geographic size, population, and economy. It is also very diverse—at least economically if not in terms of ethnicity, religion, or language. Although China does have ethnic minorities such as the Tibetans and the Uighurs, 92 percent of the population is Han Chinese. In terms of religion, the government is officially atheist, and well over half of the population claims to be nonreligious. As for language, although different communities in China do speak different dialects, Putonghua (also called Standard Chinese) is the official spoken language of the country, and the vast majority of Chinese citizens are fluent in it.

It is in the economic dimension that China is really diverse. China has one of the most unequal wealth and income distributions of any large economy on earth. According to the Chinese government's official figures, the Gini coefficient (a measure of income inequality ranging from "0" to "1") for 2012 was 0.47,[12] much higher than the 0.33 number for India and 0.39 for the United States. Unofficial figures put China's income inequality even higher. A report by a Chinese university estimated China's Gini coefficient for 2010 to be 0.61.[13]

The wide diversity in incomes means that there is no such thing as an average Chinese consumer. Per capita incomes vary dramatically across provinces. To illustrate, in 2012, the per capita income in Shanghai was about US$13,500. In the neighboring Anhui province, just four to five hours away by train, it was only one-third as much—US$4,500. In terms of corporate strategy, this economic diversity can be both a challenge and a blessing. It is a challenge in that the company may need to adapt its products and services not only for China but, within China, for different provinces and/or city tiers (Tier 1 or 2 or 3, and so forth). This adds complexity and adds to the number of strategic variables whereby the company can go wrong. At the same time, it's a blessing in that this challenge is faced by all competitors, domestic as well as foreign. Thus, for many industries, China is not one market but an amalgam of many quite different market segments. When designing an entry strategy, in the initial stage the company may not need to design a strategy for China as a whole; they can simply figure out the beachhead segment where entry barriers as well as the risk of failure are likely to be low. After getting traction in the beachhead segment, the company can then focus on migration to other adjacent segments.

Economic diversity can also manifest itself in the B2B arena. To illustrate, for a company such as TCS, the market is highly segmented not only in terms of industry verticals (such as banking, insurance, airlines, and so forth) but also in terms of the type of corporate customer (for example, foreign multinationals, central government SOEs, provincial government SOEs, large private sector companies, small and medium-size private sector companies, and so forth). This segmentation adds complexity but also makes it easier to design a lower-risk entry strategy.

Rapid Pace of Change

Aside from vastness and diversity, another challenge that companies face in China is an extremely rapid pace of change. This is due to both rapid economic development as well as the fact that the government has concentrated power and can force rapid change if and when it decides to. Rapid change means that consumer habits and industry structures often change at several times the pace of other large economies such as the United States and Europe, where Indian companies have learned the art and science of globalization. As an example, take luxury goods. As recently as 2010, even affluent Chinese buyers wanted "logo-fication" (for example, LV plastered all over the exterior of a Louis Vuitton bag) so that their friends and colleagues could see that they were carrying a top brand item. As of this writing, Tier 1 customers have come to prefer subtlety. They are more comfortable with their wealth and, having traveled to Europe, they have observed what the Europeans prefer.

Companies must also expect slower GDP growth in the future (below 7 percent rather than over 10 percent as in the past). As of this writing, the following are some of the other major changes under way in China:

- A more vocal Chinese middle class, which demands better-quality consumer goods from companies and greater accountability and responsiveness from the government
- A rising currency and rising wage levels, both of which impact cost structures
- A location shift in labor-intensive manufacturing, from coastal zones to inland provinces where wages are much lower
- A stricter pollution control regime
- Greater transparency in laws and their implementation, especially labor laws
- Rising land costs and higher local taxes levied by heavily indebted local governments

Brutal Competition

Although some industries remain highly concentrated, for many sectors competition in China is far more brutal than in most other countries such as India or the United States. China is home to about one hundred car companies, one thousand steel companies, and about five thousand cement producers. The top ten cement companies in China account for only 14 percent of the market. In contrast, in India, the top five companies account for about 50 percent of the market.

Outsiders are often surprised to find that, even in those sectors where all of the companies are state-owned, competition can be very brutal. The three telecom operators in China—China Mobile, China Unicom, and China Telecom—are all owned by the central government, yet marketplace skirmishes among the three tend to be at least as brutal as those between Coke and Pepsi. The same is true in the airline sector, where all of the big players are state-owned yet compete with each other ferociously. The Chinese government has pursued an unusual hybrid of the state and the market. Even in those sectors where the government has chosen to keep private companies out (for example, telecom operations), chief executives of the SOEs compete for promotions to more important political positions. These promotions depend at least partly on their performance in managing the company that they were appointed to lead.

Competition can be even more brutal if the various players are owned by different provincial governments. A provincial governor is evaluated heavily on the basis of how well his or her province does on the key metric of GDP growth. Achieving this goal depends directly on the performance of companies located in the governor's own province. As a result, provinces can often be found competing with each other to attract investment, technology, and jobs, with the ferocity of an economic war. Such competition among provinces can be a big plus for a foreign company trying to decide where to set up a factory.

Indian business leaders should also keep in mind that the scale of Chinese companies can often be very large. In 2012, China's GDP was four times that of India and its manufacturing sector almost seven times as large. The passenger car sector is a good example. In 2012, the total production of passenger cars in China was almost five times that of India (15.5 million versus 3.2 million). As a result, auto component companies are really mega-scale. Manufacturers in China also reap the advantages of world-class infrastructure. In addition, if the company is state-owned and has access to cheap capital and cheap land, its competitive advantage can be huge. For these reasons, foreign MNCs find it very difficult to export manufactured goods to China unless they have a technology and/or brand advantage (for example, Mercedes cars, Apple iPhones, high-end machinery). On the other hand, if a foreign company can partner with a Chinese state-owned enterprise, then it can enjoy many of the same advantages that may be available to domestic Chinese companies. In the tractor business, Mahindra Group has adopted such a strategy to great advantage.

Building on domestic strength, some Chinese companies have now become formidable global competitors. Huawei Technologies is the leading example. Founded in 1987 in the southern city of Shenzhen, Huawei has become one of the largest telecom equipment companies in the world, with 2012 revenues of US$35 billion, over half of which came from sales to telecom operators around the world. Huawei has also been one of the most globally minded large companies in China. In the late 1990s, Huawei set up its first R&D center outside China in Bangalore. This center now employs about two thousand people and is one of the most important R&D centers in the company's global network.

Other private-sector global leaders from China include Lenovo (PCs, tablets, and smartphones), Haier (home appliances), Alibaba (ecommerce and other internet services), and Tencent (gaming and internet services). Along with Naspers from South Africa, Tencent is part owner of India's ibibo (an ecommerce and online transactions company), founded by Arvind Kashyap in 2007. In June 2103, ibibo acquired redBus.in, the Bangalore-based leader in online bus ticketing in India.

Differing Priorities: Growth versus Profits

Indian and other foreign MNCs often face this challenge when partnering with a Chinese company—especially when it is an SOE. For private sector companies—be they from India, China, or elsewhere—the primary goal is to maximize revenues, profitability, and cash flow. In contrast, the primary mission of a typical SOE is to help advance the government's policy agenda rather than to maximize shareholder value. The policy agenda may include job creation, providing low-cost input to other downstream enterprises, gaining market share within China or globally, and garnering prestige for China by becoming listed in the ranks of the *Fortune Global 500* companies. The government is also able to help the SOE achieve these policy goals by ensuring that the state-owned banks provide low-cost loans to these enterprises.

If the foreign company's goals center around short-term profit maximization (including a relative quick payoff on its initial investments), then it could find itself in serious goal conflict when setting up a JV with an SOE in China. The foreign company may give primacy to profits, whereas the SOE may give primacy to growth. This is exactly the trap that the Indian auto components company described earlier fell into when it set up a JV with a prominent SOE in China. When discussing the JV in the first place, it is critical to make sure that there is alignment in the primary goals of the two partners. Otherwise, it'll almost certainly degenerate into a case of "same bed, different dreams."

Common Reasons Why Some Joint Ventures Fail

Given the complexities of a vast market like China, many Indian companies have partnered with or are exploring partnering with Chinese companies in China. A joint venture can be a very useful strategy to combine the complementary strengths of the partners. However, many companies tend to rush into these alliances only to repent at leisure.[14] Here are some of the key reasons for these failures of joint ventures:

- Lack of clarity regarding why the company needs a joint venture in the first place
- Choice of a wrong partner; that is, a partner with whom the risks of a conflict over goals, strategies, or corporate cultures are exceptionally high
- Even when a good partner is chosen, poor understanding of the partner's background, strengths, weaknesses, and reasons for wanting to do the joint venture
- Ambiguous or illogical agreements regarding board composition and decision rights regarding key management appointments and strategic decisions
- Inadequate investment of time and effort by the senior leaders of the Indian parent to build familiarity, mutual comfort, and trust with their counterparts—the senior leaders of the Chinese parent
- Inadequate investment of time and effort to build visibility and support for the JV with the appropriate government leaders at all levels—local, provincial, and central
- Ill-defined mechanisms for resolving conflicts
- Lack of predefined exit valuation methodologies and procedures

Safeguarding Intellectual Property

On the books, Chinese laws regarding protection of intellectual property (IP) are quite comparable to those in the advanced economies. The challenge is that enforcement of these laws tends to be very weak. This challenge is faced by not just foreign but also domestic companies. A company can often put in place a number of measures to significantly reduce the risk of IP theft. However, this requires that the company have its eyes open regarding the seriousness of the risks.

All aspects of the business are susceptible to imitation—from technologies to product designs to logos and brand names to even the whole package. In 2010, Apple discovered that the number of fake Apple stores in China actually exceeded the number of genuine ones. The fake stores had done an excellent job at replicating the look, logo, layout, and even the apparel of employees in Apple's genuine stores. Interestingly, the staff in some of the fake stores thought that they were working for Apple.[15]

As China has come to focus on shifting the economy's basis from imitation to innovation, enforcement is improving. Also, growing numbers of Chinese companies are becoming conscious of the importance of protecting IP. As a result, patent applications by Chinese companies within China are rising dramatically, and there has been a steady increase in the number of court cases regarding IP rights violations that Chinese companies file against each other (see "Three Types of Patents in China"). Also, two decades ago many Chinese judges were political or military appointees and ill-equipped to try technical patent cases. But as a result of better training—particularly in Tier 1 cities such as Beijing, Shanghai, and Shenzhen—this has become much less common. These trends provide encouraging signals about the future of the IP regime in China. Nonetheless, the country still has a long way to go before a company can feel secure about its IP. In the meantime, companies can implement a number of strategies to reduce the risks. These strategies center around reducing the incentive to steal IP, reducing the ability to steal IP, and minimizing the residual damage if IP theft does occur.[16]

Three Types of Patents in China

There are three types of patents in China: invention patents, utility model patents, and design patents. China follows the first-to-file rule, and all patents in China are granted by the State Intellectual Property Office (SIPO). The requirements for an invention patent are that the invention must possess novelty, inventiveness, and practical applicability. Invention patents are substantively examined and issued for twenty years. The requirements for a utility model patent are, in theory, similar to those for an invention patent. A utility model patent may be sought for any novelty pertaining to the shape and/or structure of a physical product that would have practical use. However, utility model patents undergo only preliminary examination to ensure that they comply with formalities and that there is no obvious reason for rejection. They are issued for ten years. There is no equivalent of such utility model patents in some Western countries such as the United States and Canada. Design patents protect the design of a product and are also issued for ten years.

Talent Management: Acquisition, Engagement, and Development

A major worry of operating managers in China, domestic as well as foreign, is the challenge of acquiring and managing talent. The problem is not raw numbers. China produced seven million college graduates in 2013, up from one million in 2001. The annual output of more advanced degree holders is also very large—over half a million master's level and over sixty thousand PhD level graduates in 2012, compared with less than one-fourth of these numbers in 2001. However, as in India, the challenges pertain to quality versus quantity, attracting and keeping the best talent, and ensuring that people remain engaged and productive.

- **Employee Attitudes and Cultural Issues**. Overall, Chinese employees tend to be more loyal to particular superiors than to the company. In the Confucian tradition, the role of a manager is akin to that of a leader or parent who should be followed rather than questioned. This is very different from what's typical in India, where arguments and alternatives are aired openly, which encourages creativity but slows down execution. The manager in China is expected to behave benignly, taking care of subordinates' overall needs in a somewhat paternalistic style. As in India, most employees are willing to work hard, are optimistic about their prospects in a growing economy, and take for granted that early promotions and pay hikes will come about as a matter of course. However, unlike in India, Chinese employees tend to exhibit a much higher level of discipline and tend to place much greater importance on meeting deadlines. Given the cultural importance of hierarchy, matrix structures run a high risk of failure.

- **Hiring and Retention**. Chinese employees tend to place an exceptionally high value on monetary compensation. Thus job hopping for a somewhat higher compensation appears to be common. Turnover rates among professional staff are much higher than in India, often as high as 20 to 40 percent a year. A number of strategies can help in retaining top talent. These include competitive salary and benefits, abundant engagement activities to build social bonds between the employee and the organizational community, and an active corporate social responsibility agenda on the part of the company so that people feel proud to belong to the company. If the company's plans include hiring fresh graduates from colleges and universities on a regular basis, it is important to build the company's brand in the student community. This would require regular visits to the targeted campuses and showcasing the fact that the company provides highly valued training programs. Also, China has a very large blogger/netizen population (over six hundred million at present) that is extremely active on the Internet. Corporate reputations can be easily destroyed if the company is seen as not being employee friendly or socially responsible. Thus it is important to monitor and use the power of social media both to build the corporate brand and to avoid nasty surprises.

- **Training and Development**. If it is critical to build a strong company culture and one has the luxury of time, then it is always better to grow the workforce organically by hiring fresh graduates rather than from other companies. It is less expensive, builds loyalty, and ensures that a company's global processes and ethical practices are deeply embedded in the company. Training and development programs at all levels are essential. Many companies invest in either creating their own training institutes or partnering with a local university to conduct company-specific training programs. The Chinese government spends considerable funds on skill upgrading. Many provinces provide subsidies for employee development.

- **Unions.** Large companies are formally required to have a union. With the enactment of tough labor laws, unions have become much more active in recent years. Note, however, that the government keeps a watchful eye on all union activities. Although unions do not need to seek government permission to engage in industrial action, it would be very unusual for a union to undertake action that the government disapproves of. Companies also need to create a forum for disseminating and discussing company-wide HR-related issues with staff representatives.

- **Expatriate Assignments.** Even though the bulk of the employee base in China will perforce consist of local employees, companies almost always need a small number of expatriate managers and technical staff in key positions. This could be to ensure the transfer of corporate systems, processes, and codes of conduct, disperse technical knowledge to and/or from the Chinese operations, exercise control over the local operations, ensure requisite integration between the local operations and operations in India or elsewhere, and keep the colleagues and corporate leaders in India well informed about developments in China. Sending expatriates to China generally costs much more than in many other parts of Asia because schooling and medical costs can be high. Indian expatriates generally find it easy to adjust to the Chinese environment due to the fact of an enveloping Asian cultural background. Relations between Chinese and Indian staff tend to be generally very friendly and easygoing. Often younger Chinese staff are eager to learn more about India and are interested in Bollywood and other stories about India.

Public Relations and Building a Brand

For any new entrant wishing to expand in China, brand recognition is likely to be a major challenge. The Indian company can expect to face a number of local and well-known global brands. Also, most marketing communication is in the local language rather than English. Thus building a brand from scratch is likely to be costly and will take time. The process can be shortened if you enter China by acquiring a local brand, as Mahindra did (or, alternatively, acquiring a well-known global brand—as Tata Motors did). Brand building can also be accelerated if the company is in the B2B sector and part of a well-known industrial group with a strong global reputation. Indian companies in software and IT services can also leverage India's strong brand image as a global leader in this sector.

Brand building in China should be viewed as a multidimensional task that includes cultivating the desired image with target customers, various government entities, and potential new hires. Many new entrants to China assume that, because the media is tightly controlled by the state, the use of public relations firms and advertising agencies to build a brand will have limited potential. Note, however, that although government control is exceptionally strong in the case of political news, companies are generally quite free to disseminate business-related news. The press and the public follow business and economics news widely and with great enthusiasm—almost the opposite of what is generally the case in India, where political news tends to dominate. It is not unusual for a corporate press conference to last for hours and include intense questioning from a large number of enthusiastic reporters from the print, TV, and online media.

To sum up, China offers vast and multifaceted opportunities. However, cracking the China market (or, indeed, any large foreign market) will never be easy. Those business leaders who decide to take on the challenge can significantly increase the possible rewards and reduce the risks if they remember that success in China must be viewed as a never-ending process of continuous learning. It requires humility as well as confidence. Being in China should be viewed as part of the company's long-term global strategy. Quick payoffs are rare, and going in with such expectations is almost certain to result in failure.

Leveraging India's Home-Country Advantages

Tata Consultancy Services in China

> We are delighted with the visit of the premier to our group
> and this facility. China is a very important geography for the
> future growth of the Tata Group, and we continue to increase
> our investments and scale of operations in that country.[1]
>
> —Cyrus Mistry, chairman, Tata Group

Monday, May 27, 2013, was a very important date in the
calendar of Tata Consultancy Services' (TCS) young and
widely admired CEO, Natarajan "Chandra" Chandrasekaran.
He would be hosting China's Premier Li Keqiang during his
visit to TCS's technology development facility at Goregaon,
Mumbai. The visit was significant, as it was to be the premier's
only private visit in India, and it indicated China's continuing
interest in the Indian software and IT services sector. TCS had
been both a pioneer and a leader in this sector for over three
decades.

Though Premier Li didn't know it, the groundwork for this
visit had started a decade ago on a date that, for other reasons,

looms large in world history—September 11, 2001. This was the day Chandra made his first trip to Shanghai with Girija Pande, his head of Asia Pacific—and a coauthor of this book. Deng's experiment of opening up China had been in full swing since 1978, and the rapid pace of China's transformation since then had impressed Pande. Chandra recalled that, sitting in the Grand Hyatt lounge in Shanghai's eighty-eight-floor Jin Mao Towers, he and Pande had sketched out a back-of-the-envelope strategy for TCS to enter China. Their goal was to develop TCS's foray into Asia's fastest-growing IT market—one that would soon overtake Japan, traditionally the largest market in the region. Chandra had heard about China's complexity and challenges from TCS's global customers who had ventured into China earlier. However, he and Pande believed that China held vast opportunities for TCS and had to be inherently a part of the company's global strategy.

China, TCS, and Chandra had all come a long way in the twelve years since that first trip. Now, in 2013, as the CEO of the company to which he had devoted most of his life, Chandra prepared for Premier Li's visit. It was natural to feel honored that the premier of this now-established power had made time to visit TCS. As he looked through the folders in his iPad, he could not help reminiscing about TCS's decade-long journey in the premier's country.

In the course of twelve years, TCS had expanded in China to nearly 2,200 full-time employees (of which nearly 94 percent were locals) at development centers spread across six cities. TCS China now served over forty global and domestic clients in the financial services, manufacturing, and telecom as well as government sectors. The company's key clients included Eaton, Motorola, Cummins, Bloomberg, China Foreign Exchange Trade System (CFETS, a subsidiary of the People's Bank of China, China's central bank), Guangdong Provincial Rural Credit Cooperative Union, Bank of China, China Trust Bank, Hua Xia Bank, JPMC Bank, and Mitsubishi, among others. Since its inception, TCS China had operated profitably and won many accolades, including being named the 2013 Top 10 Global Service Provider in China. It had built a strong brand in China as India's number one technology company. However, in Chandra's mind, TCS still had miles to go in a country with enormous opportunities, especially in the domestic market. He wanted to focus on the latter in his meeting with the Chinese premier.

OFFSHORING SERVICES: SAUDI HAS OIL, INDIA HAS SOFTWARE

Some countries are blessed with natural resources, as is the case with Saudi Arabia and oil. Others, such as India, are blessed with people with a centuries-old affinity for math and logic and a more recently developed fluency in the English language. These home-country advantages, coupled with the emergence of low-cost satellite communication, have made India a global power in IT services. As India's biggest IT services company, TCS has become an emblem of the country's success in this sector.

How had TCS come so far? The Indian software industry—led by companies such as TCS, Infosys, and Wipro—had emerged onto the global stage by pioneering the offshoring of software development, other information technology services, and business process outsourcing (BPO) to India. Offshoring revolutionized the way IT was delivered to large U.S. companies, making it far more cost-effective. These Indian pioneers had perfected complex software delivery processes to international quality standards and made it a very compelling proposition. It was usually said that clients came to India for cost savings and stayed for quality. India's English-speaking, young, and energetic software programmers were recognized for their mastery over software development, and many went on to become well-known founders of technology companies in Silicon Valley. Over the years, the dominance of the Indian IT sector came to be recognized globally. Well-known technology firms like IBM, HP, Cisco, and Accenture eventually followed suit and set up very large competing software development centers in India. The offshoring model has rightly earned India the title of "back office of the world."

Meanwhile, Indian software exports had grown explosively since 2000. By 2012, exports of IT services from India neared US$70 billion. India's National Association of Software and Services Companies (NASSCOM) projected this figure to grow to US$200 billion by 2020. However, this model of offshoring services had flourished mostly in English-speaking advanced countries, becoming mainstream largely among *Fortune 500* companies in the United States and the United Kingdom. Language remained a barrier in other non-English-speaking countries. China was going to be a complete outlier—a vast, complex developing country that was predominantly Mandarin-speaking and whose large corporate sector was dominated almost completely by state-owned enterprises.

In 2001, it was clear to TCS's then-CEO S. Ramadorai ("Ram") that if TCS was to become a truly global giant rather than just a leader in India, it had to enter the growth markets of Asia and Latin America—despite the language barriers. China would become a test case of TCS's global ambitions. Success in China would give the company a truly global footprint. Ram was also aware that CEOs of U.S. MNCs expected trusted service providers like TCS to go along with them as they expanded into emerging growth markets.

TCS *shi zuo shen me de?*

When Pande first went to Shanghai with Chandra, the interpreter often had to translate the question *"TCS shi zuo shen me de?"* ("What does TCS do?"). Pande's answer was straightforward: TCS is part of the Tata Group, India's largest and most respected business house, which holds nearly 75 percent of the TCS's equity capital (see "Tata Group: A Profile").

Tata Group: A Profile

Tata Group is a highly diversified group of companies that began in 1868 as a trading firm, founded in what was then called Bombay (now Mumbai) by Jamsetji Tata, an enterprising pioneer and a strong proponent of India's industrialization and self-reliance. A fundamental value of Tata Group, which remains true to this day, is a strong emphasis on ethical business conduct. In 2013, in a report on emerging market MNCs, the Berlin-based Transparency International placed four Tata Group companies in its top ranks for best-in-class transparency and ethics.

The task of growing Tata Group after India's independence in 1947 fell on J.R.D. Tata, who, during his long tenure, led the group into new areas and was awarded India's highest civilian award—Bharat Ratna—by the country's president. His successor, Ratan Tata, a graduate of Cornell University, built on this legacy and earned a reputation as a brilliant entrepreneur in tune with global trends. He led the successful globalization of the Tata Group. During 2002–2012, the last decade of Ratan Tata's tenure as group chairman, revenues grew tenfold, to US$100 billion—fuelled by acquisitions including a US$13 billion deal for the Anglo-Dutch steelmaker Corus and a US$2.3 billion purchase of luxury car brands Jaguar and Land Rover (JLR) from Ford Motor Company. In late 2013, Tata Group's market capitalization was almost US$100 billion—nearly 9 percent of the entire market capitalization on the Bombay stock exchange. TCS, Tata Group's flagship company in the information technology sector, contributed nearly two-thirds of the group's market value.

In 2013, Tata Group is India's largest business house, comprising over ninety companies in seven major manufacturing and service sectors. The group has 450,000 employees in eighty countries. Nearly 60 percent of group revenues come from outside India. Over the last decade, many of the Tata Group companies have attained global rankings in their areas of operations. By revenue, Tata Steel is the world's ninth-largest steel company; TCS, the world's seventh-largest information technology company; Tata Beverages, the world's second-largest tea company; Tata Motors, the world's second-largest company in trucks and buses; and Tata Chemicals, the world's largest producer of soda ash.

In 2012, Ratan Tata retired as chairman and handed over the reins to Cyrus Mistry, whose family owns the largest stake (nearly 18 percent) in Tata Sons, Tata Group's holding company. Cyrus Mistry has signaled that his initial focus will be on consolidating Tata Group and making the existing businesses stronger.

Tata Consultancy Services is considered the Tata Group's crown jewel. It has revenues of over US$11 billion and 280,000 employees (comprising over a hundred nationalities spread across forty countries). With a market capitalization of US$60 billion, TCS is the world's second-most-valuable IT services company after IBM (which has a market capitalization of US$202 billion), putting it ahead of rivals like Accenture (US$50 billion) and Hewlett-Packard (US$43 billion). TCS's 1,100-plus customers include many *Fortune* 500 companies. The relationship with some customers—such as American Express, British Telecom, AIG, and Citibank—goes back decades.

An industry observer recently noted that "TCS has long been the 800-lb. gorilla in the Indian offshore space but until recently has never really been able to take its rightful spot in the market, always overshadowed by the likes of Infosys and Wipro. Today, they have very clearly separated themselves from the rest of the Indian pack."[2] In recent years, TCS has leveraged its broad and deep technical and domain capabilities effectively and built up its brand among the world's largest *Fortune* 500 companies. Over the years, TCS has won many awards and accolades (inclusion on the *Forbes* list of the most innovative companies in the world and the Asian Fab 50 Companies, and recognition by both *Business World* and *Fortune India* as India's most admired company). Chandra, the current CEO, won CNBC's Asian Business Leaders Award in 2012, and Asian Investor named him "Best CEO" in the Institutional Investor's 2013 Annual All-Asia Executive Team Rankings.

TCS's Journey in China: Crossing the River by Feeling the Stones

TCS pioneered the business of writing software in India in 1968. Right up to the 1990s, the Indian market for domestic IT services was underdeveloped. As a pioneer, TCS was forced to look outward to markets like the United States and the United Kingdom, which welcomed a new low-cost quality provider of software services. By the turn of the twenty-first century, a combination of the Y2K scare, growth of the Internet, and rapidly exploding telecom bandwidth had allowed TCS to establish itself with major *Fortune* 500 companies. In 2000, then-CEO Ram became eager to go beyond traditional English-speaking markets into the growing emerging markets of Asia Pacific (APAC) and Latin America. Ram knew that this expansion would need larger investments and longer gestation. But he decided that the gamble was worth it.

In 2001, TCS embarked on its APAC journey. Girija Pande, then head of TCS APAC, was clear that no APAC strategy would be complete without a China entry. He was also familiar with the challenges of setting up operations in China. In early 2002, Pande asked an energetic TCS manager to move to China as the company's representative and survey opportunities—to *feel the stones*, as it were, *in the mighty but difficult Chinese river*. The initial survey quickly ruled out acquisitions, as the market was underdeveloped. There were a number of entrepreneur-run IT companies with little knowledge of global practices or quality standards and very high staff turnover. Moreover, it was clear that the market was so different from what TCS had seen anywhere else that it would be better to start small and learn. The services sector in China was just developing—unlike the manufacturing sector, where China was well on its way to global leadership. TCS decided to learn about China by focusing on slow but steady growth. In hindsight, this has saved TCS considerable angst and millions of dollars in write-offs. Many other ambitious global CEOs from other countries have not been so lucky, as they have made expensive acquisitions—lured by China's market potential, oversold to them by enterprising local entrepreneurs.

To start with some momentum, TCS leaned on its close connections with GE to become their first anchor client in China. GE too was looking for a trusted global IT services supplier like TCS to enter China. It sought TCS primarily for three reasons. First, GE was growing fast in China and needed someone familiar with its IT systems. Second, with its major reliance on offshoring of IT/BPO services in developing countries, GE needed to diffuse its risks by relying on suppliers in a number of geographies. It already had a high dependence on India and saw the potential of China's IT industry with its vast pool of talented software engineers, similar to India's. Third, GE was struggling in Japan, where the cost of software engineers was sky-high, and, with an aging population, availability of talent would eventually become a problem. GE had already set up a Japanese-language BPO center in Dalian, a city in northeastern China that faced Japan and was home to many Japanese-speaking young people.

GE encouraged TCS to set up an IT center in China as well. The timing was also right. Under Premier Zhu Rongji, China had just acceded to the WTO and was keen to promote foreign technology companies to jump-start the Chinese IT industry. The Chinese government started rolling out the red carpet to welcome the bigger players from India and other countries. Governors and mayors started setting up software parks as well as training programs in English and information technology. Since Premier Zhu had visited India in 2002, he was keen to replicate the Indian services model in China. He arranged for a Sino India Cooperation Office (SICO) to be set up within the National Development and Reform Commission (NDRC)—a "super-ministry" much more powerful than India's Planning Commission.

BABY STEPS: SHANGHAI, HANGZHOU, AND BEIJING APPEAR ON THE TCS MAP

In early 2002, TCS set up a wholly foreign-owned enterprise (widely known in China as a "WFOE") in Shanghai's Pudong Software Park and named it the Tata Information Technology (Shanghai) Co. Ltd.[3] The Mandarin word *ta* means pagoda. Thus, Tata translated into two pagodas and was considered an auspicious name by the Chinese. Under the rules at the time, an IT company was not permitted to use the words "consultancy services" in its name!

Shanghai was China's financial and commercial capital and housed the China headquarters of a majority of the foreign MNCs. TCS kept the initial investment low, with the idea that additional investments would be made as required. In the meantime, TCS had won a large global deal, worth about US$100 million, with GE Medical Systems, part of which had to be delivered in China. This was a lucky break and kept the China operations profitable in the early years.

After a quick survey of suitable cities, TCS decided to set up a new software development center in nearby Hangzhou, a picturesque ancient lakeside town, about three hours by car from Shanghai. Hangzhou's advantage lay in the fact that, although it was close to Shanghai, it also had a distinctly lower-cost base and better talent availability than Shanghai. Hangzhou was home to one of China's leading universities,

Zhejiang University, which produced well-trained software graduates. The city also had a local administration that was entrepreneurial and hungry for business. They went all out to woo TCS. Shortly afterward, the company also set up a representative office in Beijing. In short, TCS started operations in China with a three-city presence focused on serving its global customers, who were entering China in ever larger numbers.

Developing Vision and Strategy

TCS's vision for its China operations was to attain a leadership position, as it had done in India. The company's China-based software centers would not be isolated outposts but would be closely integrated with the rest of the global network in a 24x7 "follow the sun" global network delivery model. They would quickly achieve the same quality standards that the company had achieved elsewhere: that is, CMM Level 5 certification. They would leverage the company's global connections and workforce and, operating under a collaborative leadership, would embody the company's time-tested value systems and culture. Training in the TCS culture of ethical behavior and trust was given the same importance as training in TCS systems, processes, and certifications. Indian managers were positively surprised that newly arrived Chinese employees liked the global feel and took quite readily to the rather different TCS value systems. Various surveys indicated very high levels of staff satisfaction. In fact, for many years TCS China's staff satisfaction index was the highest across the entire company globally (which includes over one hundred nationalities). Pande took delight in quoting this fact to his surprised colleagues from India. TCS leaders in India also realized quite early on that China had talented software engineers in larger numbers than in India. With the teaching of English being given national priority, it was just a matter of time before TCS China could start accessing this very large talent pool.

TCS's entry strategy in China was three-pronged, with three clear timelines. To make it simple for its Chinese staff and customers, it was shortened as follows:

1. Horizon 1 (immediate): China for global customers
2. Horizon 2 (within two-plus years): China for regional customers from Japan, Korea, Taiwan
3. Horizon 3 (after three years): China-for-China; that is, to develop the local market, which was seen as the most difficult task, but with the best long-term potential in Asia

TCS was clear that, to become one of the top ten in IT providers in China, it would have to go through these three phases in an evolutionary but dogged manner.

Inaugurating the TCS Shanghai entity in June 2002, CEO Ram shared with the local newspapers his perspective that anyone who wants to be a long-term player in China must come to this market early. He emphasized that the IT services industry was not capital-intensive but knowledge-intensive and that the Chinese focus on foreign direct investment (FDI) would need to change, to focus instead on developing a suitable talent base.

Because of lower costs and the availability of suitable talent, the Hangzhou development center was to be the heart of TCS's operations in China. It ramped up to nearly one hundred engineers within the first year. Shanghai was to be the delivery center for high-end IT skills not generally available in Hangzhou or when there was a need to be close to a client in Shanghai. The peculiar Chinese *hukou* system (like internal visas) meant that all high-end Chinese talent flooded to Tier 1 cities like Shanghai and Beijing, and they were generally unwilling to relocate to other cities, lest their *hukou* be rescinded. This created skill shortages in Tier 2 cities.

V. Rajanna, an enterprising TCS manager who was then head of TCS Taiwan, was chosen to start the Chinese operations because of his familiarity with the China region and his ability to handle a startup situation while laying a sound foundation for the newly established entity. He rapidly implemented TCS systems, processes, controls, internationally recognized software quality certifications and standards (CMM Level 5), and recruitment and training methodologies. Of particular importance, very early he also focused on implementing a solid culture of compliance and ethical standards. That strong foundation helped TCS expand across China smoothly.

Joys and Sorrows of Early Days: Understanding China

The company's early experiences in China were eye-opening for TCS. The city administration in Hangzhou was eager to remake the city as a center for research, biotechnology, and IT services. It went out of its way to accommodate TCS in every possible way. This came as a pleasant surprise for an Indian company that was used to the considerable red tape found in India. TCS negotiated a three-year rent-free office in the local IT Park as well as other concessions relating to work permits and exemption from the business tax levied on turnover. The Chinese government offered concessional corporate tax at a 15-percent rate for IT companies, with generous exemptions for the first two years.

With its brand unknown in China, TCS was worried about its ability to attract talented Chinese software engineers. Rajanna sought GE's help. GE came forward with the services of Cathy Wu, one of their experienced HR managers, who had just relocated to Hangzhou after serving the company in China for many years. Cathy customized TCS's global HR processes and helped build the company's brand in China by participating enthusiastically in job fairs and campus recruitments. Little did TCS realize that in China many IT professionals held the Indian IT industry as a role model and closely followed well-known Indian IT companies such as TCS and Infosys on the Internet!

Meanwhile, Pande pressed the local team to remain strictly compliant with the myriads of Chinese laws and regulations. These related to areas such as Chinese company law, local and central tax laws, value-added tax on products, service tax on revenues, cumbersome laws regarding labor rights and unions, and laws regarding recruitment and compensation. The TCS China office had to master Chinese accounting standards, which were very different from those in India, as well as invoicing laws, bookkeeping in Mandarin, complex foreign exchange regulations, the ancient Chinese chop system used instead of signatures, and legal representative status and expatriate visas, all subject to sudden changes. The only way that this could be done was to hire globally known accountants like PwC, lawyers like Linklaters, and other experts who were well-versed with Chinese laws to draw up what came to be known internally as a comprehensive Compliance Manual for a new WFOE—a feat unknown in China at that time. The *Financial Times*, the global business daily, was so taken with this idea that they even wrote an article about TCS's efforts as part of building a solid foundation in a country with disparate laws and regulations. Local city officials, who were at first puzzled by TCS's strenuous efforts in this matter, were soon requesting copies of the Compliance Manual for their own offices.

In the early stage, TCS also sent twenty specialists from India to set up systems and processes for the delivery of IT services and to train newly recruited Chinese engineers. Although the Indians adapted very well socially, despite the non-English-speaking environment, they were flummoxed by Chinese cuisine. Many were strict vegetarians, something that Chinese restaurant owners could not understand, as their cuisine contained many types of meats—some of them seemingly exotic. Rajanna, who had learned the art of *guanxi* by then, met the ever-approachable vice mayor of Hangzhou. Without batting an eye, the vice mayor arranged an Indian restaurant to be opened in the city within weeks. The Indian vegetarian meals were a relief to the grateful expatriates.

TCS Creates a JV with the Government as a Partner

Late in 2004, an excited Rajanna called up Pande, who was on vacation in India, to give him the news that the central government in Beijing wanted to speak to TCS about something important. The Chinese government was inviting three leading Indian companies to submit proposals for a joint venture with unspecified entities of the government to create a large global offshoring base in China. The companies were asked to submit detailed proposals to SICO. A meeting with senior NDRC officers revealed that they considered IT to be too important to be left solely to domestic players and that China was keen to rapidly replicate India's success in software outsourcing. The Chinese also believed that cooperation between Indian software players and Chinese hardware suppliers could be a game changer.

A quick but detailed "beauty parade" put TCS ahead of the other two Indian companies, and TCS was asked to negotiate the terms of the JV. In 2005, TCS was informed that Premier Wen Jiabao would be visiting the company's facilities in Bangalore during his forthcoming visit to India. It was clear that the Chinese were interested in a strategic partnership with India's top IT firm. While there was cause for celebrations, TCS senior managers were clearly of two minds. Should they continue with the 100-percent-owned WFOE they had already set up and decline the JV option? Or should they share the pie with a government entity and form a JV in the hope of a larger overall share of the growing domestic market? There were clear advantages to having the government as the company's partner. At the same time, the Indian media had started to express concerns that TCS would be training a potential competitor.

TCS decided to pursue the strategically smarter option of aligning itself with the government and entering into a high-profile JV, something the company had never done anywhere else. Still, partnering with the government in a country where it was omnipresent was a bold move. It could go either way, as running JVs can be difficult even under the best circumstances. Would it become a case of "same bed, different dreams," as with the many Chinese JVs that had gone sour due to the JV partners' differing visions? TCS was clear about its long-term goal. In its quest to realize its third phase "China for China" strategy by going after the fast-growing domestic market, government backing as a shareholder would be useful.

JV negotiations with government representatives were exceedingly tough, and tiring. The process took eighteen to twenty months, testing TCS managers' patience but giving them helpful insights into the local partners' working methods and priorities. At this stage, TCS recruited a new CEO for China—Johnson Lam from IBM. Lam had experience in both the U.S. and the Chinese IT markets. His hands-on experience in China made him a great addition to the negotiating team. SICO finally nominated Beijing's Zhongguancun High Technology Park (China's "Silicon Valley"), Tianjin Software Park, and Beijing University as the three JV partners who would take a combined 25-percent ownership stake in the JV. Unexpectedly, SICO also insisted that Microsoft be brought in as a third partner with a 10-percent equity stake for the first three years, after which Microsoft would exit.

The Chinese side would appoint two directors (including the board chairman) and Microsoft would appoint one. TCS would appoint four directors and also nominate the CEO. The new entity would be based in Beijing. The Chinese partners nominated as the chairman Madam Song Ling, a highly regarded professor of telecom technology who had previously worked on automation projects for the Chinese government. A genial person, Madam Song believed that China had much to learn from an Indian company such as TCS.

A sticking point arose concerning the valuation of the existing TCS WFOE that was to be merged with the new JV. This was logical, as it would create a single market-facing TCS entity in China in the IT services business. Valuation norms in 2005–2006 were very different from global standards. After much negotiation, some heartburn, and some assistance from the Ministry of Commerce, TCS managed to get a satisfactory valuation. Of critical importance, TCS was able to keep FNS China—a unit of the company's recently acquired Core Banking Systems subsidiary—out of the JV and as an independent 100-percent owned entity. FNS China owned the intellectual property and was intended to serve as the company's vehicle for entering the booming banking software systems market in China.

Rolling Out the "China for China" Strategy

TCS's decision to partner with the government proved to be a winning strategy. Soon thereafter, the company's wholly owned subsidiary FNS China won one of the largest core banking system implementation deals ever awarded by the Bank of China (China's fourth-largest bank, with over twenty thousand branches) in an open global tender with a contract value of US$97 million. TCS has always been strong in the financial sector, the source of over 43 percent of group revenues. Entering the rapidly growing Chinese banking and financial markets could be a clear differentiator. The Bank of China contract was followed by many smaller core-banking systems deals that quickly established TCS as one of the largest core-banking systems providers in China. For three consecutive years, TCS was awarded the number one position in this sector in China by IDC, a leading U.S. technology analysis firm.

Concurrent with these developments, TCS China quickly set up a software product lab for both banking and insurance products to customize its global offerings in various software products for the financial sector. The company realized that the path to quick wins in the Chinese domestic market was to introduce its global products rather than just IT services. The Chinese domestic market was rapidly globalizing, and local players were keen to acquire the latest software products to help them compete with the foreign companies arriving in droves after the WTO accession by China.

More success was to follow. TCS won a critical and high-profile software project for CFETS against tough global competition. This project would create a brand-new trading platform for bonds- and fixed-income securities markets and their derivatives for the Shanghai interbank market, the nation's largest. Such a high-volume, centralized, multisegment trading platform had never been built for any country of China's size. The specifications given to TCS were to create a market two to three times the size of the New York market, as China was preparing to deepen its bond markets and planning for the eventual convertibility of the yuan. Currency convertibility was expected to make the Shanghai bond market possibly the second largest in the world. The fact that TCS successfully commissioned this project and continues to support it is a tribute to the sophistication of the Indian IT companies and how far they have travelled in their journey from being just "body shops"—as they were often referred to in the 1990s by their steadily receding Western competitors.

A Bold Move: Smart City Solutions in China

In 2010, Dong Qiqi, a veteran of China's IT industry, took over as the new CEO of TCS China. The company then decided to start developing specialized software products to address the urgent needs of Chinese cities, which were growing rapidly. The Chinese government had decided that China would use new technologies like cloud computing, mobility, and the Internet of Things to create smart cities for its growing netizen population and for sustainability purposes. TCS decided to invest US$6 million in an R&D lab to be set up in partnership with Singapore Management University. The lab would be connected to the company's R&D centers in both India and China and would create innovative software products for intelligent cities. It would also benefit from Singapore's lead in urbanization. Under Dong Qiqi's leadership, soon thereafter,

TCS China successfully deployed a low-cost "smart health" application in the Southern metropolis of Guangzhou.

Financial sector and urban software solutions were to be TCS China's two proven solutions for the growing domestic market. Having the government as a partner helped in marketing these software solutions to state-owned banks as well as city governments.

Looking Ahead: Plans for Growth

In the period 2003–2013, several IT services companies from India have focused on China and have spent time, effort, and capital in the country. The Indian IT-BPO industry currently employs approximately fifteen thousand people in China. Of these, 90 to 95 percent are Chinese employees. Despite the industry's many years of existence, they have remained focused on serving their MNC customers, with whom they feel comfortable, mostly from a single delivery center. Thus their growth has been stymied and fallen short of its potential. Besides TCS, Infosys is one of the few that have invested heavily to achieve scale in China. TCS decided early on that it would need to have a national footprint in line with its stated strategy of growing its domestic business, which would require a local presence. In 2010, the company set up an office in Shenzhen to support the offshoring of various companies in Hong Kong, as Shenzhen was located just across the border and provided ample talents and cost benefits compared with Hong Kong. Similarly, TCS chose Dalian as part of a strategy to grow its business from Japan. Tianjin, a twin city of Beijing, would serve as the major BPO center for TCS in China. The Tianjin Software Park was a small shareholder in the TCS JV and was also emerging as a major talent base that was more cost-effective than Beijing. As a result of these moves, TCS was well balanced in three Tier 1 cities (Beijing, Shanghai, and Shenzhen) and three Tier 2 cities (Hangzhou, Tianjin, and Dalian). This footprint helped optimize the cost of operations and enabled the company to be close to its domestic customers.

For the fiscal year ending March 31, 2012, TCS China recorded nearly US$70 million in revenues and an after-tax profit of about US$4 million. The company has achieved steady and profitable growth over the decade of its existence in China. Its relationship with the Chinese partners has been very cordial, and they have been very supportive of the company, even though their ownership stake was reduced to 10 percent after Microsoft's exit and the merger of TCS's WFOE into the JV. For its part, TCS has been very sensitive to its partners' needs. The company has kept them informed on all key issues and holds advance discussions with them on major issues even when such discussions may not have been necessary. Visits by senior leaders from India always include a formal visit to the partners to keep them abreast of TCS's plans globally. Ongoing surveys indicate that customer satisfaction and staff satisfaction remain high, and the key metrics of delivery quality by TCS China are comparable to and often better than those of TCS's other delivery centers globally.

As he prepared for his session with the Chinese premier, however, Chandra felt conflicted: although TCS's growth in China had been steady over the last decade, it had been below his expectations. Elsewhere, TCS was growing much faster. He was aware that the success of the Indian IT industry in China had been limited vis-à-vis the scale of the opportunity. Most of the Indian IT companies primarily serve Western MNC customers in China and other North Asian markets. Only one or two companies have spent time and effort, like TCS, to develop the domestic market. It was also clear that, with the strengthening of the Chinese yuan and the recent weakening of the Indian rupee, the balance of software exports would tilt back to India. MNCs who were offshoring to China could be tempted to reverse their plans and start increasing their reliance on India.

The lack of opportunities in the big-ticket domestic deals within China that TCS had won in other markets was creating difficulties for Indian IT companies, and Chandra wondered if he should raise this issue with Premier Li. How might Indian IT companies become bigger suppliers to large and dominant Chinese SOEs?

Chandra was also aware of another perennial problem that the industry faced in China: much higher staff turnovers than in India. Globally, TCS was well recognized for its best-in-class talent management practices. Outside China, the company's turnover rate averaged around 11 to 13 percent. However, in China, it hovered between 20 and 28 percent, despite the company's adopting global best practices and winning many national and provincial awards related to human resource management. Surveys within TCS China routinely indicated high levels of staff satisfaction. Part of the problem related to demography and the availability of experienced middle management. Also, as a result of the one-child policy, the younger generation has grown up as princelings, doted on and pampered by six people—two parents and four grandparents. Their expectations are higher, and they become restless more easily. For this knowledge-intensive industry to grow rapidly in China would require building an adequate talent base.

A lot had been accomplished, but much remained. Chandra hurriedly prepared talking points for his forthcoming meeting.

4

Making China a Second Home

Mahindra Tractors in China

China is the best thing that happened to India. Now we can say to the politicians, "Look, this is our competition, this is what they're doing. Why aren't we?" It's something to whip up our competitiveness. China is the benchmark.... For a country that invented yoga, the science of stretching, we just didn't stretch ourselves.[1]

—Anand G. Mahindra, chairman and managing director, Mahindra Group[2]

The story of Mahindra Tractors in China is one of ambition combined with discipline and a willingness to learn. Along with the automotive sector (which focuses largely on SUVs), tractors is one of the two core businesses of the Mahindra Group. It is also the one that gives the group a market leading position not just in India but, in terms of number of tractors sold, globally.

Mahindra Tractors entered China in 2005 through a relatively small 80:20 joint venture with the Jiangling Tractor

Company, a state-owned enterprise. In 2008, it followed up with a much larger 51:49 joint venture with the Jiangsu Yueda Group, another state-owned enterprise. As of 2013, these operations give Mahindra a roughly 9 percent share of China's tractor market—behind First Tractor Company, Foton Tractor, Changzhou Dongfeng, and John Deere. The first three are Chinese state-owned companies; the fourth is the well-known U.S. giant in agricultural machinery.

The leaders at Mahindra Tractors believe that they are gaining ground in China. They view China as a second home market and have begun to voice their ambition to capture the number three slot in China's tractor industry within the next five years.[3]

THE MAHINDRA GROUP

As of 2013, the Mahindra Group is a US$15.9 billion revenue corporation, making it one of India's leading industrial houses. The group was founded in 1945 as a steel trading company. In 1947, it entered automotive manufacturing to bring the iconic Willys Jeep to Indian roads. In 1963, Mahindra Group diversified into tractors. Since then it has also entered other businesses, such as information technology, financial services, and hospitality. The group's two biggest businesses are automotive and tractors. In 2012, autos accounted for 55 percent of the group's revenues and 24 percent of profits before interest and taxes. The tractor business made up 22 percent of the group's revenues but a much heftier 39 percent of profits.

Mahindra Group is led by family scion Anand Mahindra, the grandson of one of the company's founders. He joined the group in 1981, soon after completing an MBA from Harvard; he became president and deputy managing director in 1989, managing director in 1997, and chairman of the board in 2012. Under Anand Mahindra's leadership, the group has come to be defined by several key features: the company's brand premise, a federal structure, the "Blue Chip" mantra, going global, and inorganic growth.

In talking about his perspective on the group's brand premise, Anand Mahindra observed:

> A brand is not something that's plucked out of thin air. A brand has to be based on what you really are and what you really do . . . Whenever we build a rugged off-road vehicle, we not only make a profit, but we also help a rural entrepreneur in India or Egypt or South Africa build a shared transport business, and we help the villagers who use it to acquire mobility . . . We want to be the brand that works alongside our customers to help them achieve their own goals. . . . So our brand purpose more or less proclaims itself—"Mahindra Helps You Rise"—because when you rise, your community rises, and we rise with all of you.[4]

Bharat Doshi, Mahindra Group CFO, explained how the federal structure works and makes the group different from a conglomerate:

> The group today comprises eleven businesses with about forty-five operating companies. Each business sector is autonomous, and some of these even have separate listed companies. Often the investors and analysts ask, "How do

you manage these multiple businesses?" Some ask why a conglomerate discount should not be applicable to the sum of the parts. Our response is that the Mahindra Group today is not a conglomerate. It is a federation of businesses. The investors now have the option to invest in the parent company or they can invest directly in the listed subsidiaries or associates, thereby investing in a specific business.

This distinction is relevant because a conglomerate does not provide this option . . . The group, though being large, with its federal structure, provides autonomy to its constituents, who with independent management can still remain focused and nimble to operate in the marketplace. At the same time, the federal structure ensures that this web of businesses and companies has a binding thread—the core values of the group.[5]

Around 2002, Mahindra Group launched Operation Blue Chip. Driven by the belief that you must be strong at home before you can play on the global stage, the Blue Chip initiative was aimed at strengthening the company's domestic operations across a number of dimensions—innovation, market leadership, and working capital management. This initiative also placed far greater emphasis on free cash flow and return on capital employed (ROCE), the goal being to build a war chest to finance global expansion through acquisitions.

Corporate leaders believed that success at acquisitions depended heavily not just on deal-making skills but also on leveraging the group's culture and internal processes. As a result, they developed strong investment banking capabilities in-house and preferred to do the deals themselves rather than rely on external investment banks.

MAHINDRA TRACTORS

Mahindra entered the tractor business in 1963, setting up International Tractor Company, an India-focused joint venture with International Harvester of the United States. The collaboration with International Harvester continued until 1971. In 1977, International Tractor merged with Mahindra & Mahindra to become its tractor division, and in 1982 the group launched Mahindra branded tractors. Soon thereafter, Mahindra became the leading tractor brand by market share in India—a position it has held ever since.

Mahindra focuses primarily on small- and medium-horsepower tractors, the largest market segments in India. In 2004, the company enjoyed a 26-percent market share in India distributed primarily across 21- to 50-horsepower tractors. Other Indian companies captured bulk of the remaining market. Global competitors such as John Deere and Case New Holland, although established in India, focused largely on the above-50-horsepower tractor segment and were viewed as niche players.[6] In 2007, Mahindra acquired Punjab Tractors, the number two player. As of 2012, Mahindra was the clear leader in India, with a market share of about 42 percent generated by tractors in the 20- to 80-horsepower range.

In 2003, Mahindra Tractors won the Deming Prize for quality, making it the only tractor manufacturer in the world to have won this award. The company's core competencies centered around strong internal systems and processes and skilled manpower, both of which gave it an advantage in terms of quality and cost leadership.[7]

The tractor business has also served as the launchpad for Mahindra Group's globalization. India is the world's second-largest market for tractors but only one of the top ten in autos. Also, Mahindra is India's market leader in tractors but not in autos. Thus, in the tractor business, Mahindra is able to leverage its India-based scale and cost advantages on the global stage to a far greater degree than would be the case in the auto business. It is also important to note that, compared with passenger vehicles such as SUVs, tractors are much more a functional rather than an emotional product, so the lack of a strong brand image in foreign markets presents less of a barrier for marketing tractors.

Until the early 1990s, global expansion meant exports from India—first to neighboring markets such as Nepal, Bangladesh, and Sri Lanka and then to other emerging markets in Latin America and Africa. A major shift took place in 1994 when Mahindra Tractors set up a small manufacturing plant in Texas. In 2002, the company set up a second U.S. assembly and distribution center in Calhoun, Georgia.

In 2005, Mahindra Tractors entered China through a JV with Jiangling Tractor Co. This was followed in 2008 by a much larger JV with the Jiangsu Yueda Group. Since 2011, Mahindra Tractors has been the world's largest tractor company by volume. It sells more than 240,000 tractors annually in more than forty countries and has manufacturing operations in India, China, the United States, and Australia. It occupies a niche but respected number six position in the U.S. market and is the fifth-largest tractor company by market share in China.

In July 2006, *BusinessWeek* praised Mahindra tractors in a cover story on "Emerging Giants." The magazine quoted Jamie Lucenberg, a farmer from Mississippi, who needed to buy a tractor to clear debris from his seventeen-acre family farm in the wake of Hurricane Katrina: "I have been around equipment all my life. But, for [US]$27,000, complete with a front loader, the 54-hp Mahindra 5500 is by far the best value for the money. It has more power and heavier steel. When you lock it into four-wheel drive, you can move 3,000 pounds like nothing. That thing's an animal."[8]

WHY CHINA? WHY 2005?

As a key element of his growth strategy for the group, Anand Mahindra often talked about his desire to stay in only those businesses with the potential to go global. The tractor business had emerged as the most promising of all. In fact, the senior leadership had long believed that they must aim for global leadership in this sector. This would require having a solid position, if not the leading one, in every big tractor market in the world—including China.

The seeds of the group's ambitions in China were sown in 1999 when Anand Mahindra hired Anjanikumar Choudhari as president of the Farm Equipment Sector. Choudhari knew China well from his 1994–1999 stint as sales director for

Unilever China and as vice chairman and managing director of Unilever Shanghai Sales Co.

The Chinese tractor market bore some important similarities to the Indian market. The market for wheeled tractors was almost as large as India's. Also, as in India, the average farm plot in China was quite small (although many state-owned farms could be very big).[9] Thus, unlike in developed markets such as the United States, Europe, or Australia, the bulk of the demand in the Chinese market was for small (less than 100 horsepower) and inexpensive tractors. Choudhari reasoned that Mahindra might well have a better shot at tapping into this opportunity than rich-country players such as John Deere.

Even though China's total land area is more than three times that of India (9.3 million square kilometers versus 3.0 million square kilometers), the amount of arable land is much smaller (1.1 million square kilometers versus 1.6 million square kilometers). Also, given the Chinese population's rapidly rising incomes since 1980, their eating habits have been changing rapidly. The increase in meat consumption has meant increasing demand for animal feed and thus for grain. These developments have made ensuring food security and controlling food price inflation among the most important policy priorities for the Chinese government.

As a result of these factors, the Chinese government has undertaken a series of ongoing reforms in the farm sector—all aimed at the twin goals of boosting agricultural productivity and freeing up farm labor to staff the rapidly growing manufacturing sector. In the period leading up to 2005, these measures included the following:

- Permitting farmers to rent or lease their land rights to others, thereby enabling farms to become larger
- Reducing and eventually eliminating taxes on agricultural production
- Direct subsidies to farmers for planting grain
- Direct subsidies for purchase of seeds and machinery
- Increased spending on rural infrastructure (irrigation facilities, electricity, roads, and the like)[10]

In addition to these moves, around 2004 it was also becoming clear that the government's eleventh five-year plan beginning in 2006 would not only continue agrarian reforms but also ramp them up. Looking at these developments, Mahindra Group's corporate leaders concluded that the tractor market in China would almost certainly see rapid growth, and that any further delay would be a costly mistake. China needed to become the company's second home.

ENTERING CHINA

Mahindra Group's first foray into China was to explore the potential for exporting tractors from India. The team quickly realized that India-made tractors were far too expensive for the Chinese market. Harish Chavan, president of the company's China operations in 2012, elaborated on the reasons why:

> For the same horsepower, the tractors that we were trying to bring from India were at least twice as costly as those available locally. In many parts of China, the usage of tractors—in terms of days in a year—is much more limited than in India.

For example, in northeast China, the winter is very severe and the tractor may get used for only forty days in a year. In other parts of China, they may have two crops in a year and thus higher usage. In India, the tractor is generally used for the entire year. As a result of these differences, the reliability requirements in many parts of China are very different from those in India. There is also a usage difference between the two markets. In India, tractors are used on the farm as well as for transportation and haulage by attaching a trolley to the tractor. But in China tractors are used only on the farm. As a result of all of these factors, even though customers liked the product from India, it was just too expensive and totally uncompetitive.[11]

The Mahindra team quickly concluded that the only way to compete in China would be with a locally designed and manufactured product. Based on his experience in China, Choudhari argued that this meant working with a local partner rather than setting up a 100-percent-owned greenfield plant.

At that time, most of the tractor manufacturers in China were state-owned enterprises. With some exceptions, most were relatively small, single plant operations. Because of these factors, their lack of sophistication, and the burden of pensions, many were also in financial difficulty. As a result, the central government as well as many local governments welcomed privatization and consolidation of the tractor industry.

The industry also appeared ripe for development on all fronts—technology, production quality and efficiency, dealer network, and after-sales service. For example, almost all dealers had franchises for multiple brands, and the concept of after-sales support was largely nonexistent. Reflecting the heritage of a planned economy, the entire industry appeared production driven rather than market driven.

In its search for a JV partner or acquisition target, the Mahindra team zeroed in on Jiangling Tractor Company (JTC), a relatively small tractor company that was in difficulty and whose current owners were eager to find a new partner. JTC was a unit of Jiangling Motor Company Group (JMCG), a state-owned enterprise with US$1 billion revenue based in Jiangxi province, whose main business was light trucks and buses. Ford Motor owned a 30-percent stake in JMCG. In 2002, JMCG had financed the construction of a new production facility for JTC, with an annual capacity of ten thousand tractors (in the 18- to 33-horsepower range) and three thousand engines. Yet, as of 2003, given JTC's high cost structure, capacity utilization was a tiny 15 percent. The company's work force of 710 was also about twice as big as needed. JTC's revenues accounted for less than 1 percent of the parent company revenues. Given all of this, both JMCG and the Jiangxi government were eager to exit from the tractor business.

The Mahindra Group agreed to do an 80:20 deal with JMCG whereby it would pay US$10 million for 80-percent ownership of JTC. The acquisition price included an up-front payment of US$2 million and a commitment to invest another US$8 million to turn JTC around. There would be a ten-member board, made up of Anand Mahindra and seven other people from the Mahindra Group plus two people from JMCG.

In the early period after the closing of the deal, Choudhari described his team's assessment of JTC:

> There is good chemistry with management and we are comfortable with their straightforward management style, degree of cooperation and level of assistance. This is important because our partner is the government which has given us permission to come here in the first place.[JTC's] Feng Shou brand has a good reputation in the small tractor market in China. The company's product range is complementary to [ours]. There is an internal focus on quality and readiness to employ [our] quality practices. JTC is a government enterprise and willing to give us full control of day to day management.
>
> We [also] saw areas of concern. JTC's product range was limited to 18–33 hp. The company's manufacturing locations were far away from the markets. Capacity was a constraint, especially in engines. A majority of the dealers were ineffective.[12]

The Mahindra team also felt that JTC's plan to exit from the domestic Chinese market and concentrate on exports was inconsistent with their own strategic intent. For them, the bigger game was to go after the Chinese customer. The domestic market was growing rapidly, and they wanted to establish a leading position before it became mature.

The company's decision to target a relatively small player reflected a strategy to treat this as largely a learning move. Other than Choudhari, who had lived and worked in China for five years, almost all other members of the team had very little experience in China and viewed the country as a bit of a mystery. Thus the team decided to take a low-risk approach and to treat the JTC acquisition as the necessary first step on their learning journey. This experience could also serve as the basis for a bigger move later on. The logic was that they would not learn about the market unless they went there.

Harish Chavan reflected on why it was better to do a JV rather than a 100-percent acquisition:

> Before we took any decision, we sent a team to stay there for six months, study the market, and figure out possible entry strategies and possible follow-on strategies. The study led to the conclusion that we need to go for a joint venture, and we started the search for a partner. This was absolutely the right decision.
>
> Of course, unlike in some other sectors, such as wind turbines and new energy, the central government does not have any industrial policy aimed at promoting national champions in the tractor industry. Yes, there's a subsidy. However, this is paid to farmers rather than to tractor companies. In that sense, domestic and foreign companies are treated similarly. However, at the local level, domestic companies can have an indirect advantage. Since we have the local government as our partner, we are able to benefit from these local advantages.

TRANSFORMING JTC

Once the 80:20 joint venture deal was completed, Mahindra Group changed the name of the new company to Mahindra China Tractor Co. Chavan recalled some of the key decisions and early experiences:

> We brought in the CEO from India. Below him, we had two senior managers—a CFO and an operations general manager. The CFO was also from India, while the operations general manager was Chinese. All of the other functional heads—for sourcing, manufacturing, product development, quality, sales, and HR—were also local. We did bring in some Indian managers below a few of the functional heads—in sales, sourcing, and quality. These mid-level Indian managers were our eyes and ears on the ground, and they helped us learn about the operations and the market. They also played a key role in providing support to the implementation of our systems and processes.

After some time, however, the company decided to bring senior managers from India to take charge of quality and sales. As Chavan explained:

> We did not replace the Chinese managers. Rather, we brought in the Indian managers in more senior roles. We wanted to strengthen the company's operations significantly in all aspects of marketing and after-sales service, such as proper brand management, bringing discipline to the sales channel, and a much stronger focus on customer service. In every one of these areas, we wanted to move away from a

commodity approach and build a differentiation advantage for us. These also required a stronger focus on quality in sourcing and manufacturing. Our Chinese colleagues did value quality. However, their approach to achieving quality relied heavily on gut-level decisions. We felt the need to infuse our approach based on data, systems, and processes.

You have to be careful about managing the change and also the timing. Expats are very expensive. When the operation is small, you cannot afford to bring in too many expats. Also, the goal must be that after two or three years you would not need so many expats. You also have to be very careful in selecting the types of expats that you bring. They should be people who can make a difference while treating their Chinese colleagues as peers rather than acting like bosses. They have to make sure that the Chinese colleagues don't feel as if they're losing their identity. So we brought people who were doers rather than just trainers, who could do things with their own hands and show what a difference a new process can make. I am very happy to say that the Chinese colleagues have caught up extremely well.

One also has to remember that the cultural differences may not necessarily be at the national level; that is, Indians versus Chinese. Instead, the differences could simply be due to the type of company that you are. We're a private sector company, and JTC was a state-owned enterprise. Thus one has to be sensitive to the factors that may lie behind the differences and not jump to hasty and superficial conclusions. We were also lucky that we did not have any case of an expat not working out. Many had experience in other countries. But this was their first assignment in China.

For the Indian expatriates in China, language was initially a big challenge. Chavan elaborated on how the company handled this:

> We had to learn how to overcome the language barrier. We encourage people coming from India to learn Chinese and our Chinese managers to learn English. Of course, we support them in this process. All of our people who've been here for some time are now able to communicate in Chinese. Still, that doesn't mean that they can communicate in Chinese anything close to how they can communicate in English. So we use panel boards a lot. When an Indian expat is making a presentation, we have them write the key ideas and any decisions that have been taken and any directions that they want to give on the panel board. Another person translates these simultaneously into Chinese. This approach of both verbal and written communication helps enormously in ensuring that people understand each other.

A second major initiative focused on the development of higher-horsepower tractors. With the ongoing consolidation of farms and the new agricultural policy, the tractor market was growing at an explosive rate. It grew from 56,000 units in 2003 to 222,000 units in 2008—an average annual growth rate of 32 percent. Moreover, bigger farms needed higher-horsepower tractors. The managers at Mahindra China Tractor went flat out to develop a 55-horsepower tractor in just eighteen months.

These developments—both internal and external—helped boost the company's output from about 1,500 units in 2003 to over 5,000 units in 2008. Although the trend was in the right direction, corporate leaders felt that a 2.5-percent market share in China was just too small to give the company the needed scale either to compete effectively in China or to help the group achieve global leadership in the tractor industry. Having learned from four years of experience with this smaller acquisition, they now felt ready to make a bigger move.

A SECOND JOINT VENTURE IN CHINA

In August 2008, Mahindra Group signed a second joint venture agreement in China—this time with Jiangsu Yueda Yancheng Group, a state-owned enterprise based in the Jiangsu province bordering Shanghai. With revenues of about US$7 billion, the Yueda Group was one of China's one hundred largest business groups (and one of the top ten in Jiangsu province). Like the Mahindra Group, it operated in a diverse set of businesses including automotive, coal, infrastructure, real estate, and textiles as well as hotels and supermarkets. Many of these subsidiaries were joint ventures with partners such as South Korea's Kia Motors, Japan's Fuji, France's Carrefour, and Germany's Triumph.

The transaction became official in February 2009. Mahindra Group invested US$26 million to acquire a 51-percent stake in a JV, the Mahindra Yueda Yancheng Tractor Company. Yueda Group contributed all of its tractors-related assets and liabilities in return for a 49-percent stake. Both sides agreed that Mahindra Group would appoint the CEO. While the CEO would report to the JV's board of directors for all major decisions, Mahindra Group would have effective operational control. The chairman would be Chinese; the vice-chairman would be Indian.

For the year 2007, Jiangsu Yueda's tractor operations produced twenty-six thousand units, which included exports of eight thousand units to the United States and generated revenues of about US$120 million. Sold under the brand name Huanghai Jinma, the product range was 16–125 hp, much wider than that of Mahindra China Tractor. At the inauguration of the new joint venture in January 2009, Anand Mahindra shared his perspective on the potential synergy between the two partners:

> I have always believed that India and China have unique and complementary strengths, which, when pooled together, can take on the world. We already have a successful joint venture with Jiangling Tractor Company. This JV between M&M and Yueda Group will further combine Indian entrepreneurial and managerial skills with Chinese competitiveness and efficiency. I am sure this formidable combination will contribute substantially towards realizing our ambition to be the leading tractor manufacturer in the global market.

Hu Youlin, chairman of Yueda Group, echoed Anand Mahindra's views:

> This JV stands to gain by the operational excellence, international sales and distribution network and R&D capabilities of Mahindra and the distribution competence and manufacturing strength of Yueda and will eventually lead to the creation of China's leading tractor company.

A few months later, Bharat Doshi, group chief financial officer at Mahindra, noted that the cost of manufacturing a tractor was at least 25 percent cheaper in China than in India. The main contributor was logistics cost, as China's "infrastructure is substantially better." He also speculated that, as a result of these cost differences, the company may be exporting as much as 30 percent of its China production in five years' time.[13]

During 2009, the first year of the new joint venture, Harish Chavan and his team concentrated on improving the systems and processes in a number of areas—sales planning, order management, and the monitoring of inventory and retail sales on an ongoing basis. They introduced new systems for dealer sales forecasting and annual sales planning and launched initiatives to improve customer contacts. To bring discipline to the channel, they also systematized credit policies and introduced dispatch control. On the export front, to improve profitability they started promoting direct exports rather than selling through trading houses. With respect to operations, the new management set about to reduce the breakeven point by addressing all aspects of costs. They introduced new systems for monitoring trends in raw material prices and standardized methods for cost reduction. On the organizational front, the new team set about creating a new culture that would leverage the strengths of both parents. These efforts included establishing more performance-focused but also more employee-friendly HR policies.

In November 2009, the two partners agreed to make a fresh investment of US$40 million in the JV toward setting up a new R&D center as well as a new engine manufacturing plant and modernizing the existing manufacturing operations. The engine plant would manufacture more fuel-efficient, more reliable, and lower-emission engines and thus create a differentiation advantage for Jinma tractors. The investment in manufacturing would help consolidate all manufacturing of Jinma tractors in one location and, through modernization, boost both productivity and quality. These moves were enthusiastically encouraged and supported by the government of Yancheng city, where the JV was based. Chavan explained the logic behind developing the new engine:

> Currently, the engine is a commodity in China. Many tractor companies in China don't necessarily make their own engines. In contrast, every tractor company in India makes its own engines. As a result, in China, two competing tractors could have the same engine. We believe that the engine can be a differentiator. Mahindra is well known globally for making very fuel-efficient tractors. It's part of the company's core proposition. Having your own engine is critical to delivering on this core proposition.
>
> In the first phase, this engine will cover the 30- to 95-horsepower range. Even though we make engines in India in this power range, we decided not to bring the Indian engines to China. Instead, we went out to develop a completely new engine. We needed to factor in manufacturability considerations as well as some unique customer preferences. Our goal was to not only meet but actually beat the fuel efficiency and reliability standards that we get from engines in India. The design team included experts from both India and China. We

wanted to leverage the expertise from both sides and also to make sure that the new engine could be manufactured in both China and India.

On September 6, 2011, Mahindra Yueda Yancheng Tractor Company laid the foundation stone for the construction of a new engine plant.

As of 2012, the market for tractors in China stood at about 360,000 units (versus about 480,000 units in India). The top two players, First Tractor Company and Foton, both state-owned enterprises, controlled market shares of about 20–21 percent each. The third player was Changzhou Dongfeng, another state-owned enterprise, with a market share of 12–13 percent. John Deere, with its two subsidiaries, came in fourth with a market share of 12–13 percent. Adding up the sales of its two joint ventures, Mahindra ranked number five, with a market share of about 9 percent.

Looking ahead, Pawan Goenka, president, Auto & Farm Equipment Sector for Mahindra Group, noted:

> The company has made a huge progress in China and we are number five in terms of volume. Our objective is to become the third largest tractor manufacturer in China within the next three to five years. Our current volume is around 35,000 units a year and it will have to be doubled, if not more, if we are to become number three in China.[14]

Partnering with Chinese Institutions

NIIT in China

W e help the Chinese youth to achieve their potential, aspiration and ambition to play a leading role in the global IT space. . . . We are [also] ambassadors of Chinese youth and are trying to help them understand the strengths of India and China and develop a mutually beneficial partnership between the two countries.

—Vijay K. Thadani, cofounder and CEO, NIIT Limited[1]

A global leader in talent development, NIIT has thrived in China; as of 2013, it was training over 30,000 information technology professionals each year at more than 140 centers. NIIT China has won many accolades from Chinese institutions, including several bestowed in 2009 by the Chinese Society of Educational Development Strategy (CSEDS, a unit of the central government's Ministry of Education):

- The most influential IT training brand in China
- A top ten brand in China's overall training industry

- A top ten brand in student placements in China's training industry
- The most influential brand in franchising in China's training industry

At the awards ceremony, CSEDS also honored Prakash Menon, president–NIIT China, with a Celebrity Award for influencing the development of the training industry in China.[2] Menon is widely regarded as the dean of Indian company CEOs in China. Based in Shanghai, he has served as the president of NIIT China since 1997, making him the longest-serving head of any prominent Indian company's Chinese operations. In making NIIT a success in China, Menon has had enthusiastic support from Rajendra Pawar (chairman) and Vijay Thadani (CEO), who cofounded the NIIT Group in 1981 (see "NIIT Group: A Profile").

NIIT Group: A Profile

Founded in 1981, NIIT Group presently comprises two entities—NIIT Limited, which focuses on training and education, and NIIT Technologies, which focuses on information technology solutions. Both companies are listed separately on the major stock exchanges in India. For the fiscal year ending March 31, 2013, NIIT Limited and NIIT Technologies reported revenues of about US$300 million and US$400 million, respectively. This profile focuses on NIIT Limited, the training and education company.

NIIT pioneered the computer education market in India, creating a completely new industry segment and leading it to consolidation and maturity. Early on, the company's founders realized that the rapid growth of India's software and services industry would create a massive need for trained manpower—a need that the country's universities and colleges would be unable to meet, for several reasons. First, although formal degree programs may be good at teaching computer languages, these programs were not set up to impart a number of behavioral skills essential to becoming a successful IT professional. Second, hardware and software technologies keep evolving rapidly. Thus IT professionals need to keep mastering the latest technologies continually. Third, in terms of sheer numbers, the growth of industry needs would far exceed the pace at which the formal university and college system could scale up.

Since its founding, NIIT has broadened the scope of its training solutions and services. Today the company defines itself as a global talent development corporation that serves four distinct market segments across forty countries, including not only India and China but also the United States and many other countries in Asia, Africa, and other continents. The four business units, each serving a distinct market segment, are

- *Individual Learning Solutions*, targeted at individuals, with the goal of creating or enhancing their employability. The bulk of the opportunity for individual learning solutions is in emerging markets.

- *Corporate Learning Solutions*, targeted at companies, with the goal of creating custom learning solutions and managed training services. The bulk of the opportunity for corporate learning solutions is in developed markets.
- *School Learning Solutions*, targeted at school systems and private schools, with the goal of providing multimedia teaching and learning content as well as teacher training. The opportunity for school learning solutions cuts across both emerging and developed markets.
- *Skill Building Solutions*, NIIT's newest line of business, aimed at helping the Indian government transform millions of unskilled youth into readily employable professionals across a number of industry sectors including IT, media and entertainment, retailing, hospitality, health care, and so forth.

Over the years, NIIT has earned recognition not just in India but also in many other countries. For example, NIIT India was recognized as India's Most Trusted Education Brand by Brand Trust Report in 2013. NIIT Vietnam has received the ICT Gold Medal from the Ho Chi Minh City Computer Association for several consecutive years. And NIIT USA ranked number three overall and number two by size of deal in *HRO Today* magazine's 2012 Baker's Dozen Customer Satisfaction Ratings for Top Learning Providers.

As part of its ongoing innovations in learning content and methodology, NIIT recently launched India's first cloud-based campus. Because it should be more flexible and scalable at a lower cost, the NIIT Cloud Campus is expected to enable the next phase of growth for the company worldwide.

We have followed NIIT's evolution in China for several years and had many discussions with Prakash Menon. During late 2012 and early 2013, we conducted a series of interviews with him to document this evolutionary journey in greater detail. We also visited one of the larger NIIT centers in Wuxi. This chapter summarizes the key aspects of this journey. The primary lessons that emerge from NIIT's experience pertain to

- The importance of being open to learning rather than staying rigidly committed to what works back home or in other countries
- The importance of local adaptation
- The central role that partnering with government institutions can play in helping a company succeed in China

ENTERING CHINA

By the mid-1990s, the Chinese economy was growing rapidly, and it was anticipated that China would soon be joining the World Trade Organization. This would lead China to open its economy further to foreign companies and to begin playing by international rules. In 1997, NIIT's Pawar and Thadani dispatched Menon, one of their enterprising senior managers, to China to explore what the company could do. The thinking was that NIIT could enter either the education or the software and services space, its two main lines of business.

Menon proposed targeting the education space. At that time, out of the one million students completing college degrees each year, only fifty thousand were being trained in IT—an extremely low number for a country whose economy was growing by 8 to 9 percent per year. It was also clear that Chinese youth had high aspirations and wanted to move up and do bigger things. When Menon looked at the universities, he concluded that they were not geared, even remotely, to creating IT professionals. In the four-year degree programs the content was extremely weak, in terms of both the number of hours dedicated to the subject as well as what was being taught.

There were small private institutes that were doing four- or five-day programs. However, nobody was building the computer professional of the future. Knowing a language like C++ is not enough. The professional must also be able to use a structured problem-solving method to take a bigger problem, break it down into smaller problems, and then solve these one by one until the bigger problem is solved. The professional needs to be good at all aspects of the cycle—requirements analysis, architectural design, coding and implementation, verification and documentation, and maintenance. Nobody was teaching this entire cycle. People also needed behavioral training in areas such as working effectively in a team, completing assignments on time, making a decent presentation, and communicating effectively. All of these are part and parcel of a programmer's life. A person may start as a junior programmer but eventually can move on to become a senior programmer, then a designer, then an analyst, and then a project manager. As the person climbs through the ranks, the repertoire of necessary skills becomes much broader than those needed to be just a good programmer. As Menon recalled:

In 1997, who was attempting to train the IT professional in China? Nobody. There were a couple of American companies. They too were just teaching technologies. Also, they did not quite understand China. The books were in English and the pricing was atrociously high. I went to the supermarkets and to McDonald's to learn how much the average person spends. I studied what people were buying, how they negotiated. It became obvious that price points were extremely important.

I also met up with the heads of a lot of companies. I'd just walk into their offices and say, "Hi. Help me understand China." They shared with me whatever little bit they knew. I began to feel comfortable that maybe we have a story that we can develop in China, where we can build a computer professional. I knew we were good at it. We knew exactly what to do, and we had done it in many other countries. Then came the big questions: Should an Indian company train the Chinese? Are we creating competition for ourselves? I faced these questions back home. My answer was—look, it's not as if the Chinese are waiting for us to train them; they will do it anyway. And you have the Americans here, you have everybody here. So what are you waiting for? Let's engage with China. At least you would know what is going on. You would be better prepared.

Pawar and Thadani gave Menon the go-ahead. The next question for NIIT was how to get a license to start offering courses. The company retained a global consulting firm and went calling on the city governments in Beijing and Shanghai. The Beijing government was not particularly receptive to the idea of permitting a private sector company to start offering a two- to three-year nondegree program. In contrast, the Shanghai government was a bit more receptive and willing to experiment. After some back and forth, the city government agreed to a ten-year contract between NIIT and the Pudong Continuing Education Centre (PCEC), a unit of the Shanghai Education Bureau. The agreement with PCEC gave NIIT permission to start teaching in just one center in Shanghai. The company rented space on Nanjing Road, the most famous street in Shanghai at the time, and got going. Menon described what happened next:

> In collaboration with J. Walter Thompson, we ran a series of ads in Shanghai newspapers that said, "It doesn't matter if you're a black cat or a white cat. All that matters is whether you're a smart cat." We did a spin on Deng Xiaoping's famous statement and proposed that, if you want to be a smart cat, come to NIIT. After the ads started running, more than two thousand people showed up inquiring about our courses in the first week itself. We never expected such

144

a response. Every process that we had built came crashing down. We realized that we were understaffed and our processes were inadequate. So in the first batch we admitted about four hundred people. We admitted two more batches shortly after that, and we had about a thousand students studying in that one center.

Soon after the ads came out, the Shanghai Ministry of Education called asking how the company could use Deng Xiaoping's statement for commercial purposes. Menon invited them to visit the center. When they saw the youth of Shanghai so eager to take NIIT's courses, they let the company be. It also helped that, even at that time, India was doing well in IT and was well regarded. The Chinese were receptive to the idea that, since this was an Indian company, these folks must have something to teach the young people. Another important factor was that, in this space, the Chinese felt that NIIT was not eating off of their plate. And education and training were not seen to be as commercial as other activities.

In the beginning, there was skepticism about whether people would sign up for a two- to three-year-long nondegree program, especially as NIIT was an unknown brand. But people did sign up. The company's ads seemed to have succeeded in capturing the imagination of young Shanghainese. There were also many discussions about pricing, particularly since people would be paying for the program from their own pockets. Menon proposed charging 4,000 RMB per semester. Others felt that this was too high and would not work because the targeted students could not afford it. This fee was about three times that charged in India, in line with the fact that per capita incomes in China were three times those in India and the company's costs in China were higher. NIIT attempted to help the students by giving them the choice of paying in monthly installments, thereby reducing the burden of having to pay all of the fees up front. However, eight months down the line, Menon decided to discontinue the installment approach because many students simply chose not to pay the installments. Menon elaborated:

> The fact that the person knows he has to pay you means that he also knows that you'll dance to whatever he says. Our life became all about chasing money. It also became awkward because this is a relationship between an institution and a student, and now we have to keep thinking about how to get paid. We didn't want to be acting like a bank chasing credit card defaulters. It messes up the relationship. So we discontinued the installment plan. Now, you have to pay the entire fee up front at the beginning of the semester. There's a one-week no-penalty drop-out period. But, after that, if you drop out, you don't get any fee back.

MANAGING INTELLECTUAL PROPERTY RISKS

For NIIT's leadership team in China, this was a period of massive learning on all fronts, including how to protect intellectual property (IP) such as logo, brand name, course material, and the like. It was obvious that the company would have to rely on Chinese trainers in order to conduct the courses in Chinese. They would also have to translate all of the teaching material into

146

Chinese. Menon recalled how he and his colleagues managed the translation of the textbooks into Chinese:

> We hired fourteen professors to localize our textbooks. We knew about the intellectual property risks in China. So we never gave the whole book to any one professor. We broke it into fourteen parts and gave a different part to each professor. Localization also meant more than just translation. For example, in India, we use cricket as a common example. That won't work in China. So we had to substitute that with something locally relevant. Also, take a simple word such as "classroom." At NIIT, we call the classroom a mind room. Now, what's the Chinese word for mind room? That was a challenge. We also had to make sure that the fourteen translators would use the same words and phrases when doing the translation so that the end result would be cohesive rather than disjointed. So we had to create our own private dictionary. These are all examples of the time, effort, energy, and talent that went into localization.

The company also asked a Chinese lawyer for advice on how to minimize the intellectual property risks. The lawyer proposed a seemingly novel idea—make innocuous but deliberate mistakes in your course material. That way, if the mistakes are copied and NIIT takes the violator to court, there will be no ambiguity that the other party is at fault. This approach proved successful, and, to this day, NIIT China continues to make deliberate mistakes in its course material. The subject matter itself (that is, information technology) has also created an automatic safeguard. In IT, things change all the time. As a result, the content must also change constantly. If someone wants to copy NIIT's text material, they face the ongoing challenge of having to do it over and over again as versions are updated. This is very different from a subject like chemistry, with its enduring principles. As Menon put it, "If I was marketing instructional material in chemistry, I would not want to be in China, because in chemistry things don't change as rapidly as in IT."

As with companies in most industries, NIIT has found that protecting intellectual property in China requires being on guard—constantly. Pirates have copied NIIT's logo and text material. The company has also seen complete NIIT centers spring up unexpectedly, like China's fake Apple stores. As a result, NIIT China and its lawyers now police the marketplace regularly to keep track of any fake NIIT centers that may show up. The Chinese subsidiary has been forced to build up a fairly large system to minimize IP theft, something NIIT has not needed to do elsewhere in the world.

ADAPTING TO LOCAL IMPERATIVES

Despite NIIT's long and successful experience in India and elsewhere, the China team soon discovered that their instructional methodology was failing. They knew that it could not be the content. Students were smart and had the requisite technical aptitude. After some brainstorming, they concluded that how the Chinese learn is different from how the Indians learn. In India, the company's approach was to start with concepts and then move on to applications. The Chinese students appeared to be uncomfortable with this approach.

Menon invited instructional research teams from India and Singapore to visit China and help find a solution. Their recommendation was to adopt a completely different methodology for teaching: Do the reverse of what works in India and elsewhere. Start by teaching the students how to solve specific problems. Here's a problem, and this is the solution. Here is another problem, and here's a different way to solve it. And so on. This inductive approach clicked. Over time, students also began to grasp the underlying concepts.

Human resource management was another area where Menon and his Indian colleagues had to learn quickly. In the beginning, they started by implementing long-established policies that had worked well in India. On employees' birthdays, they would get a day off and a celebratory check. In the case of married employees, their spouse would get a check on the wedding anniversary, again to celebrate the occasion. In the case of unmarried employees, they would get a check on any day that they wished to take a special friend—or an old uncle or a neighbor—out for dinner. Menon soon discovered that these and myriad other similar policies just fell flat in China.

People asked me why the company needed such a complicated system. Why not just give us money in a more straightforward manner? I also noted that everybody would leave promptly at 5:30 P.M. That seemed like a bad sign. I wondered whether there was something wrong with the way I was managing the Chinese staff. I decided to sit with them, eat with them, and talk to them a lot. I felt as if I was becoming Chinese myself. Yet the problem persisted. They would still leave at 5:30 P.M. Finally, a young female colleague helped me understand what was going on. She said, "Prakash, why should we work beyond 5:30 P.M., because you would pay us the salary anyway?" That hit me. The next day, I changed the HR policies. I said, "OK, from now on, only 50 percent of your salary is fixed. The rest would be variable based on performance. If you achieve 80 percent of the goals, you get 100 percent of the variable part, and that'll bring your take-home pay to 20 percent higher than the industry." It worked. Now, we have the reverse problem. Nobody goes home. Everybody stays back because they now have the reverse pressure. My conclusion is that, in China, it's very important to have clear rather than complicated, hard-to-understand policies. Also, money is a much bigger driver of motivation in China than in India.

I also learned that if employees feel that they are being taken care of, they become extremely loyal to the boss. Instead of seeing him or her as someone to be feared, they begin to see the boss as a coach and mentor. In such a case, they will fight for you and will not let you down. On the other hand, building loyalty to the organization, over and beyond the direct boss, takes longer and depends on what the organization stands for, where it is headed, and whether it instills pride among the employees.

SPREADING WINGS BEYOND SHANGHAI

The first batch of students from the center on Nanjing Road graduated in the year 2000, and almost everybody received an attractive job in Shanghai. This was an eye-opener for the city government. The NIIT model did not need any campus, the government was not spending any money, yet people were being trained in IT and getting good jobs. Menon felt that it was time to start spreading the company's wings. NIIT applied for permission to set up a wholly foreign-owned enterprise (WFOE) that could set up franchise operations throughout China. A WFOE status would free the company from dependence on the Shanghai government contract and enable it to start opening centers in other cities.

The government officials were perplexed as to how one could franchise education. How, for example, do you clone a professor? NIIT explained that their entire approach to training rested on almost complete standardization of the content as well as delivery methodology. As such, it was much closer to McDonald's than a typical university. Once the officials understood what NIIT did, how it operated, and how this approach had worked well in the center on Nanjing Road, they agreed. NIIT China (Shanghai) Limited came into being and began to look for franchisees.

The year 2000 was important for NIIT China in another respect as well. Because of the dot-com bust that year in the United States, NIIT USA faced serious financial challenges. As Menon recalled, the company's cofounders informed him, "Look, from here on, you're on your own; don't ask for any more money." On the one hand, this constraint meant that NIIT China would now have to generate its own cash flow to finance future expansion. On the other, it meant that Menon now had an even freer hand to take an entrepreneurial approach to NIIT's expansion in China.

The journey has turned out well. NIIT has continued to expand in China, with more than 140 centers as of 2013, and Menon has not felt the need to ask his bosses for any more capital since 2000.

As NIIT discovered, however, getting permission to start franchising did not automatically translate into finding franchisees. As had been the case with NIIT back in 1997, each franchisee needed a license from the city government. In the educational sector, this was not easy, as the city governments were determined to ensure that the students would not be fleeced. NIIT looked around to check who already had the licenses. The answer was clear—the universities and colleges. Consequently, NIIT decided to see whether they might be interested in signing on as franchisees. They were. The success in Shanghai served as a credible evidence of NIIT's effectiveness. The academic institutions also boasted excellent infrastructure, including plenty of classrooms and computers. Much of the time, the infrastructure sat idle or, in the case of computers, was used by the students for gaming. The university administrators could see that becoming an NIIT franchisee would enable them to generate fresh revenues from these idle resources at no extra cost.

For NIIT, signing on universities as franchisees solved two major problems. First, universities already had the licenses to offer educational programs. Second, unlike private entrepreneurs, universities already had the requisite infrastructure and would not need to make any new investments. Thus, on both counts, universities could get going much more rapidly. The biggest challenge for NIIT was to figure out how to train the trainers at the universities. The most difficult thing of all was to train the professors to teach NIIT material the NIIT way. Professors believed that they already knew how to teach. And over the years, their teaching habits had become almost hardwired.

INVENTING THE "NIIT INSIDE" MODEL

Once the universities had the benefit of experience as NIIT's franchisees, some of them approached the company with a particularly novel idea. What about embedding the NIIT curriculum into their own bachelor's degree programs? The universities could see that the graduates of the franchise centers were receiving excellent training and had no difficulty whatsoever securing attractive job offers. In contrast, their own degree students did not do as well on the placement front. If NIIT's curriculum and instructional methodology could be embedded in the university's own degree programs, it could broaden the win-win partnership between the two organizations.

These discussions were the genesis of what eventually became the "NIIT Inside" model. The university would continue to teach all of the other courses—math, physics, history, literature, you name it. However, all of the IT curriculum would be taken out and replaced by NIIT's curriculum, to be taught by NIIT-trained instructors. In addition to their regular tuition, students paid an additional fee to the university. Upon graduation, they received the university degree as well as a certificate from NIIT.

The "NIIT Inside" model has proved extremely successful. Menon notes, "There are about 1,750 institutions of higher learning in China. We currently have partnerships with less than 10 percent of them. So we still have a long runway ahead of us." *Notably, NIIT Limited has now taken the "NIIT Inside" model, invented in China, to many other countries, including India.* Initially, the company was unsure whether Indian universities would embrace the "NIIT Inside" model. However, after more than a year of ongoing discussions, many of them seem to be coming around.

CHALLENGES WITH ENTREPRENEURS AS FRANCHISEES

In contrast with NIIT's success with universities as franchisees and/or embedded curriculum partners, the company found it challenging to work with independent entrepreneurs, even when the latter could get a license from the city government. There were several reasons. First, unlike universities, which were not interested in stealing NIIT's intellectual property, entrepreneurs often were. Thus they posed greater IP risks. Second, many entrepreneurs were too keen to "save a buck" if they could. Thus, after the initial honeymoon, many showed little respect for NIIT's systems, processes, and procedures. Third, once an entrepreneur-franchisee became successful and too big in a city, he or she would start renegotiating the contract with NIIT. At this point, the entrepreneur knew who had the economic power. NIIT had not faced these issues with entrepreneur-franchisees anywhere else. However, in China these became serious issues. Menon elaborated:

> I went and spoke with the CEOs of Western fast-food chains in China to find out how they managed franchisees. That's when I realized that, for similar reasons, many of them don't work with franchisees in China but run their own outlets. I stopped signing up fresh entrepreneurs as partners. The only exception would be when we control the operations in a big city. In that case, we could take on an entrepreneur as a franchisee in an outlying area. Such a situation is not very risky, because we have the power.

PARTNERING WITH GOVERNMENT INSTITUTIONS

The city of Wuxi, about an hour from Shanghai by high-speed train, provided NIIT with an early experience of how driven Chinese government officials could be about pursuing economic development. Menon recalled:

> We had a franchise operation with an independent entrepreneur in Wuxi. We did not have much choice, as Wuxi is not a big college city. One day, in 2006, the mayor called me in for a meeting and said, "I know that you have a franchise operation here. We want you to come and run your own center. What do you need?" I said, "If we have to run our own center, we need 8 classrooms, 240 computers, tables and chairs, so on and so forth." He asked us to give him a design and a bill of materials. Two weeks later, he

called me in and said, "Here's the building and the space you need. We've already fitted it out as per your design. It's completely free of cost, and there'll be no rent. Just come and run your center." We went in and started training.

Exactly one year later, his office called me and said that the mayor would like to meet us in our office. This is generally unheard of, because you go to the mayor's office, not the other way round. When he arrived, he said, "It's good that you're training 1,800 people. We also know that you have a 98-percent job placement track record, much better than our universities. Can you train 10,000 students? What would you need? Give me a detailed design in one week."

That week, I hardly slept, as I was working with the architect day and night to finalize the design. After I gave him the design, it took the city just three weeks to construct a brand-new six-floor building with thirty thousand square meters of floor space and ninety classrooms, complete with all internal fitting out, the computers that we needed, the works. Later, the mayor also set aside several million yuan that could be given to financially needy students as tuition subsidies. This is a perfect example of how I've seen public-private partnerships work in China.

An article in *China Daily*, the leading English-language newspaper, sheds light on why the government officials in Wuxi felt the urgency to partner with NIIT to develop a large pool of IT talent in the city:

Inspired by the *New York Times* bestseller *The World Is Flat*, senior officials of Wuxi, Jiangsu province, are poised to make the city China's Bangalore. Yang Weize, secretary of Wuxi's

Party committee, reiterated the commitment to develop the city into China's leading outsourcing center at a recent seminar in Beijing, where 23 projects were signed between Wuxi and outsourcers from home and abroad. . . .

Last September, the Wuxi Taihu Lake protection zone was approved as the national outsourcing demonstration zone jointly by the ministries of science, commerce, education and information industry. . . . The city's government [has] set an ambitious target to have 100 companies providing international service outsourcing and exporting software by 2010. According to the plan, each company will employ at least 2,000 staff and will have an export volume over \$30 million. Thus the total output value of the city's outsourcing industry is expected to amount to \$3 billion by 2010. "Wuxi's target of international service outsourcing should not only be a beautiful dream. We have to figure out how to realize it," Yang says.[3]

The central government's strategy to grow the economic contribution of the services sector meant that the transformation of Wuxi was not an isolated case. Government officials in other regions of China faced similar imperatives. As word spread of NIIT's successful partnership with the Wuxi government, the company started receiving invitations from officials in major cities such as Chongqing, Chengdu, and Dalian as well as provinces such as Jiangsu, Shandong, and Fujian. NIIT's partnership with Chongqing, a megacity with a population of around thirty million, was typical of these partnerships. In September 2007, NIIT CEO Thadani signed a memorandum of understanding (MOU) with Wang Yang, secretary-general of the Chongqing Communist Party, whereby NIIT would work with the Chongqing Information Industry Bureau to build human capital infrastructure for the city. NIIT would train the faculty at universities and colleges and embed its curriculum within these institutions under the "NIIT Inside" model. The company would also set up its own independent NIIT center to train those who had already graduated from the universities and thus were not part of a formal degree program. As a signal of the importance of this partnership, the government also honored Thadani by inducting him as an economic consultant to the city of Chongqing.

Another important development ensued when Menon received a call from the Party secretary of Jiangsu Province, bordering Shanghai and one of the richest provinces in China. *Xinhua Daily* quoted Li Yuan Chao, the Party secretary: "Cultivating software talent with good English communications skills would be the key differentiator for growth of the IT industry [in Jiangsu]."[4] Menon elaborated:

> Mr. Li said, "I need you to train a hundred thousand people in IT in the English language within five years." I replied that I'd need a lot of information to develop a plan. He asked if I could stay through the night. By 9:00 P.M. the same evening, he had assembled the provincial heads of the Education Bureau, the Labor Bureau, and the Commercial Bureau in his office. We talked, and by 12:30 A.M. I had the information that I needed. Five days later, I went back with a plan whereby we would bring faculty from India. They would teach English for two semesters and then IT in the English language for the next several semesters.

158

It was unbelievable. The faculty members who went to the cities in Jiangsu became ambassadors for not just NIIT but also India. Towards the end of the program, we organized an India Week. Every evening, we had films, music, cultural shows, singing, and dancing. Then we sent the best twelve students to India for a two-week period. We paired each Chinese student with a student from NIIT in India. The Chinese students spoke a bit of English but the Indian students spoke no Chinese, yet they became buddies. Several of the Chinese students ended up staying in the Indian students' homes. On the penultimate day, we had a dinner with the Chinese ambassador to India. The Chinese students sang Indian songs, and the Indian students sang Chinese songs. The ambassador was moved and remarked, "Prakash, when will you bring a million Chinese to India?" Afterwards, many of the Chinese parents called me to say that this was one of the most memorable experiences for their son or daughter.

REACHING FOR THE SKIES

Building on the company's rapidly growing reputation with not only employers and potential students but also key players in the government, NIIT is now increasing the scale of its ambitions in China. As labor costs keep rising at a double-digit pace, and the yuan continues to appreciate vis-à-vis the U.S. dollar and the euro, China is beginning to lose its historical advantage in manufacturing. As a result, the country's leaders are eager to shift the economy's basis from exports to domestic consumption, from low-tech to high-tech, and from manufacturing to services. As part of this transformation, they have launched a number of special economic zones (SEZs) focused specifically on the services sector. One such SEZ is to be based in Hainan, an island off China's southern coast.

In 2012, as part of the "Strategic Economic Dialogue" between India's Planning Commission and China's National Development and Reform Commission, NIIT submitted a proposal to help the Hainan-based SEZ develop the needed human capital infrastructure. In November 2012, NIIT signed an MOU with the Hainan government for a multiyear, large-scale talent development project starting in 2013. The company's first training center in Hainan was up and running by the first half of 2013. This project had the potential to become really big, with a contract value running into several hundred million dollars. As he looked ahead, Menon observed:

> The IT training market in China is expected to keep growing at well over 20 percent a year. Sectors like IT and IT-enabled services, business process outsourcing, healthcare, retail, and banking and financial services are set to witness massive growth as well. Herein lies the problem—where will the skilled manpower needed to fuel growth in these sectors come from? The fact that NIIT understands Western thinking, and at the same time is well entrenched in the Chinese market, has proved to be a significant edge for us. NIIT will continue to focus on developing talent for global needs, leveraging the manpower resources these two leading Asian economies offer.

6

Driving Indirectly
into China

Tata Motors and Jaguar Land Rover

Which country does Tata Motors earn most of its revenues from? The answer is no longer India, nor is it the UK, HQ to Jaguar Land Rover (JLR), the marquee brand Tata Motors acquired in 2008. It's not even Europe, another strong market for JLR. And the US is only fifth in line. In FY 14, Tata Motors is likely to earn more revenues from China than from any other country or region.[1]

—Lijee Philip, *Economic Times*, August 20, 2013

Tata Motors' success with Jaguar Land Rover in China illustrates the power of án indirect route from India to China. At the country level, India does not enjoy a particularly strong "national brand" in automobiles the way it does in, say, information technology. Further, as a company, Tata Motors has not been particularly successful in passenger cars, even though it is India's market leader in commercial vehicles. In fact, in recent years it has been losing market share to Maruti Suzuki and Hyundai, the two big players in India's auto sector. Outside India, Tata Motors has become famous for the Nano, a marvel of frugal engineering. However, the Nano has failed to excite customers in India or elsewhere—at least so far. Given all of these disadvantages, it would be almost impossible to imagine how Tata or any Indian company could ever enter China's car market and succeed. Yet, as the Jaguar Land Rover story illustrates, Tata Motors has done it—and has been extremely successful.

Today's era of global mergers and acquisitions offers an ambitious company from any country the chance to overcome what may appear to be almost insurmountable barriers to enter a demanding and highly contested new market. Look at South African Breweries (SAB), for example. In 1987, SAB was a domestic beer company confined to its homeland by the anti-apartheid sanctions imposed by the rest of the world. Today, as SAB Miller, it is the world's second-largest beer company, with operations spread across seventy-five countries. It is the second-largest beer company in the United States, the second-largest in India, and, via a joint venture, the largest in China. Virtually all of this global expansion has been accomplished through cross-border acquisitions. As another example, consider Yildiz Holding of Turkey. When it comes to premium chocolates, one normally thinks of countries such as Switzerland and Belgium, not Turkey. Yet Yildiz today is one of the world's leading chocolatiers. In 2007, Yildiz acquired Godiva, a leading premium chocolate company, from Campbell Soup Company. Leveraging Godiva's Belgian heritage, the Yildiz subsidiary is now expanding rapidly in

China, where it has opened more than fifty exclusive retail outlets that sell not only the company's global products but also specialties such as Godiva-branded mooncakes crafted especially for the Chinese market.

Take the case of Sany Group, China's leading construction machinery company. Sany has operated in India since 2002. From its manufacturing base in Pune, Sany sells machinery not just in India but also in other markets, including the rest of South Asia, Southeast Asia, and the Middle East. In 2012, Sany acquired Putzmeister, the well-known German maker of high-tech concrete pumps. As a Chinese brand, Sany machines often sell at lower prices than those by Caterpillar and Komatsu. However, Sany now has a respected German brand in its portfolio. The Putzmeister brand has enormous potential to significantly accelerate the pace at which Sany is able to expand its market position, market share, and profit margins in India as well as other countries. Similarly, consider Bright Food, China's second largest food company, which operates in many segments of the food industry including dairy products, bottled water, sugar, rice, meat, and candy. Given the vast differences in the eating habits and preferences of Chinese and Indians, it may be hard to imagine how Bright Food could hope to succeed in India. But in May 2012 Bright Food acquired a controlling stake in Weetabix Limited, a British breakfast cereals company. With the strong influence of British eating habits on Indian tastes (and vice versa), it will likely be much easier for Bright Food to enter India not directly from Shanghai but indirectly via Northamptonshire in the United Kingdom, the headquarters of Weetabix. In a similar example, Geely Holding Group, the Chinese car company, may not find it so easy to succeed in India by bringing in Chinese cars and selling them under the Geely brand name; however, should it choose to do so, Geely would have a much easier time succeeding in India via Volvo Car Corporation, the Swedish company that it acquired in 2010. As it does elsewhere, Volvo enjoys an exceptionally strong premium brand image in India.

Consider also the case of Apollo Tyres from India. China is now the world's largest market for new car tires as well as a rapidly growing market for replacement tires. Notwithstanding Apollo's strengths within India, it is unclear whether Apollo has the technology, brand, or scale advantages to leverage for a direct assault on the Chinese market from India. An indirect route, however, holds much greater promise. In 2009, Apollo acquired Vredestein B.V., a Netherlands-based manufacturer of high-performance tires. Vredestein is considered a premium brand in the automotive tire industry. Should Apollo decide to exploit the Vredestein technology, brand image, and Dutch heritage to penetrate the Chinese market, the path is likely to be easier (although by no means easy) compared with a direct route from India. In 2013, Apollo also signed a deal to acquire the U.S.-based Cooper Tire, which owns a controlling stake in a tire venture in China. This acquisition has been called off, but had it gone through, it would have given Apollo a ready-made market position in China's domestic market.

In the rest of this chapter, we present the story of Tata Motors' roaring success in China, a success achieved by leveraging the company's British subsidiary, Jaguar Land Rover.

We begin with a brief overview of Tata Motors and Jaguar Land Rover.

TATA MOTORS' ACQUISITION OF JAGUAR LAND ROVER

Tata Motors started life in 1945 as the Tata Engineering and Locomotive Company (TELCO), a manufacturer of locomotives. In 1954, TELCO started a strategic alliance with Daimler-Benz to manufacture commercial vehicles for the Indian market. Although the collaboration ended in 1969, Tata continues to be India's market leader in commercial vehicles. In 1991, Tata entered the passenger car business, launching the Tata Sierra and later a number of sedans and SUVs including the Tata Estate, Tata Sumo, Tata Safari, Tata Indica, and Tata Nano, the world's cheapest car. In 2004, Tata acquired the South Korean Daewoo Commercial Vehicles Company, now called Tata Daewoo. In 2005, it acquired a 21-percent controlling stake in the Spanish bus and coach manufacturer Hispano Carrocera, later converted to 100 percent. Tata Motors also has a Brazilian joint venture, Tata Marcopolo Bus, to manufacturer buses and coaches, and a construction equipment manufacturing joint venture with Hitachi. In 2008, Tata Motors acquired Jaguar Land Rover from Ford Motor Company. In 2012, it entered the combat vehicle business in collaboration with a unit of the Indian government. For the fiscal year ending March 31, 2013, Tata Motors reported revenues of US$34.3 billion and as of this writing ranks 316th in Fortune magazine's 2013 list of the world's 500 largest corporations.

Jaguar and Land Rover are iconic British brands with long histories. The precursor of Jaguar Cars began in 1922 as the manufacturer of motorcycle sidecars. However, since 1935 Jaguar has been known for premium sports saloons (sedans) and sports cars that reflect a unique British style. In contrast, Land Rover stands for premium all-terrain vehicles that exhibit simplicity, strength, and durability. The first Land Rover, Series I, was produced in 1948. Land Rover is widely viewed as the first company to have introduced the concept of SUVs to the world. Ford Motor acquired Jaguar for US$2.5 billion in 1989 and Land Rover for US$2.7 billion in 2000. Under Ford, both brands were managed as part of the Premier Automotive Group, which included other brands such as Aston Martin, Volvo, and Lincoln. On June 2, 2008, Tata Motors became the new owner of Jaguar and Land Rover by acquiring these two companies for US$2.3 billion, less than half of what Ford had paid for them.

Soon after the acquisition, many both inside and outside the Tata Group wondered whether even the "discounted" price that Tata had paid was worth it. The world was plunged into the worst economic malaise since the Great Depression. Although every industry suffered, the luxury auto sector was among those most affected. For the period June 2008 to March 2009, JLR reported a loss of £306 million and also suffered from a serious cash crunch. Tata Group's approach to managing JLR during this period has become the stuff of automotive industry history. They implemented a comprehensive stabilization and transformation plan that included financial support and selective cost reduction combined with ongoing investment in new product

166

development and brand building. Organizationally, Tata leadership gave JLR executives far greater autonomy than had been the case under Ford. The results have been stellar. For the fiscal year ending March 31, 2013, JLR reported profits after tax of £1.2 billion derived from revenues of £15.8 billion. With Tata Group's support, JLR continues to pour fuel into the engine. During 2013 itself, JLR is expected to spend almost £2.75 billion on new product development. Tata and JLR have been lauded not just by analysts on Wall Street (as well as Mumbai's Dalal Street) but also by automotive reviewers in influential media. The following comments by Dan Neil, a reviewer for *The Wall Street Journal*, are typical:

> Tata's rajahs have maintained a hands-off approach—at least that is what JLR executives tell me—supporting the companies financially while letting the lads and ladies in England sort out vehicle design, procurement, production and sales. Which they have done, brilliantly. The latest example is the new Range Rover Sport (base price, $63,495). . . . Would the Sport be half as good if Ford still owned JLR? Maybe. But it might also have been a gloriously reskinned Explorer, another cash cow in Dearborn's thundering herd. I like the way things turned out.[2]

Aside from excellent guidance by JLR executives and effective oversight by the Tata leadership, the Land Rover portfolio has also benefited from favorable market trends. SUVs are the fastest-growing segment in the car industry worldwide. Within this segment, luxury SUVs are growing even faster than SUVs overall. These trends are particularly positive for Land Rover, which has long enjoyed the cachet of being the most upper-crust brand among SUVs. According to an industry analyst quoted by *The Wall Street Journal* in February 2013: "Range Rover doesn't have any real competition as a super premium luxury SUV and is more often compared with the luxury limousines of German car makers such as Mercedes S-class, BMW 7 series and the Audi 8. We think it will be a long time before Jaguar Land Rover faces a real threat to its luxury SUV—at that price point it has the whole market to itself."[3] Pertinently, this article also included the following observation from Phil Popham, operations director at Jaguar Land Rover: "We were the first SUV back in 1970 and our job is to maintain the number one position by investment in the development of new products."

JAGUAR LAND ROVER IN CHINA

JLR's China journey so far has been a play in three acts. Act One covers the period from 2003, when Ford started importing Land Rover into China, until 2008, when Tata Motors acquired the company from Ford. Act Two covers the period from 2008 to 2013 under Tata ownership. This period saw an aggressive and comprehensive buildup of JLR's marketing, sales, and service network in China. Act Three will start in 2014 when JLR commences domestic manufacturing in China via its joint venture with Chery Automobile. The JV was formed in 2012, and the plant is currently under construction.

Entry into China Under Ford Ownership

Virtually every major car company in the world operates in China through a 50:50 joint venture with Chinese partners. When China joined the World Trade Organization in 2001, it was able to negotiate certain exceptions for the automotive and other sectors. Under these agreements, the Chinese government retained the freedom to require that foreign car companies could not own more than a 50-percent equity stake in an assembly operation in China. The government also retained the freedom to impose a 25-percent duty on cars imported into China. These stipulations have meant that, with the exception of luxury cars, it is virtually impossible for any foreign car company to compete in China by importing cars into the country.

In the context of these rules, Ford Motor Company formed its first passenger vehicles joint venture in China in 2001. This was a 50:50 manufacturing JV with Changan Motor Corporation (at that time, China's third-largest domestic car company after First Auto Works and Shanghai Auto) and was based in Chongqing, a megacity in central China. The plant was up by 2003, with an initial focus on compact and mid-size cars, to be sold under the Fiesta and Mondeo brands, respectively. In 2003 Ford also started selling Land Rover SUVs in China by partnering with independent Chinese importers. The imported SUVs were targeted at the upper crust of Chinese car buyers. Import duties and various other taxes meant that the retail price of a Range Rover was about 1.4 million yuan or US$166,000.

In 2004, Ford also started importing Jaguar sports cars into China. During the period 2004–2008, Ford's China strategy with both Jaguar and Land Rover was to work with independent importers who would be responsible for setting up dealerships and taking care of all sales and service functions. In terms of direct responsibility, Ford focused primarily on brand marketing. For calendar year 2008, the last year under Ford ownership, JLR sales in China were about 12,500 units, mostly from Land Rover SUVs. During that year, Jaguar recorded worldwide sales of 65,000 units, whereas Land Rover sales added up to 187,000 units.

Tata Motors Takes Charge

Soon after the change of ownership on June 2, 2008, Tata Motors found itself confronting the Great Recession and a sharp fall-off in the demand for both its luxury brands worldwide. The years 2008 and 2009 were particularly challenging. Along with the development of a stabilization and transformation plan for JLR worldwide, Tata and JLR executives also undertook a major review of the company's strategy in China. By late 2009, they had finalized the new roadmap. In February 2010, Ralph Speth, a German executive who had earlier worked for BMW and Ford, took charge as the new CEO of Jaguar Land Rover. Shortly thereafter, Bob Grace, a British veteran of JLR, moved to Shanghai as the new president of JLR China.

The company's new strategy in China was to become far more aggressive on all fronts. Compared with BMW and Mercedes Benz, JLR had been slower to ramp up in China. Making up for lost time would require determination, investment, and transformation. The first big move was to shift from relying on independent importers to JLR's own national sales company. Before this transformation, JLR had worked with four independent importers—based in Dalian, Beijing, Shanghai, and Shenzhen—that covered the entire east coast from the high north to the deep south. At this time, there were forty dealers, mostly owned by the regional importers.

After the transition to a wholly owned national sales company, Bob Grace pursued a multipronged strategy to make the company's marketing, sales, and service network wider, deeper, and more professional. During the period from July 2010 to December 2012, the new developments included

- Expansion in the dealer network from 40 to 151. Of these, 106 were in operation by the end of 2012, with the remaining 45 scheduled to be up and running by the middle of 2013. The 151 dealers would cover 72 cities all over China, including the central and western regions of the country, whose economies were also beginning to grow at very rapid rates.
- Implementation of a common information technology infrastructure across the entire dealership network—that is, a standard dealer management system and a standard customer relationship management system across all dealers.
- Establishment of training academies aimed at improving the sales and service skills of people employed by the dealers. In 2012, over six thousand dealership-level staff went through a variety of training programs run by these academies.

- Improving the dealers' ability to work synergistically with JLR on brand marketing campaigns.
- Establishment of a number of customer-focused "Land Rover Experience Centres." Open year-round, each center would partner with a five-star luxury resort and allow current owners and potential customers to experience firsthand what a Land Rover could do in off-road environments.

In a 2011 interview, Bob Grace reflected on the company's strategy behind these moves:

> Quality after-sales service drives repeat business. We have a clear plan. We are investing in the infrastructure. We are recruiting dealers and dealer groups of the highest caliber. I am very confident that the infrastructure we are developing today will stand us in good stead in the years to come. We will definitely be seen, here in China, as being a company with two great British brands which delivers great products that are very reliable and for which the ownership experience is second to none. In 10 years' time, our company will look back at this period as being a major turning point in our history.[4]

These moves might have come to nothing if the folks in Britain were not busy developing and manufacturing new cars that would wow potential customers. Fortunately, they were. In 2011, JLR launched Range Rover Evoque, one of the most successful SUVs in the company's history. Designed to appeal to urban buyers, the Evoque was lauded by auto reviewers and sold nearly eighty-eight thousand units in the first year of production. *Motor Trend*, the American magazine, declared it "SUV of the Year" for 2012. JLR launched the Evoque in

China in 2011 and gave it a Chinese name—Jiguang (polar light). The company soon found itself inundated with orders. Customers were even willing to wait several months to receive their vehicle.

Figure 6.1 tracks the history of Jaguar and Land Rover sales in China as well as the rest of the world. By any measure, JLR's

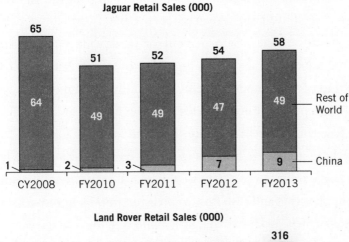

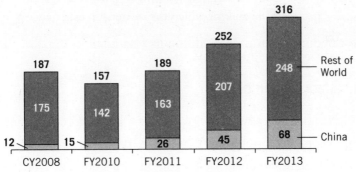

Figure 6.1   Jaguar Land Rover Sales in China and Worldwide*

Source: Jaguar Land Rover investor presentations.

*"CY" refers to Calendar Year ending December 31. "FY" refers to Fiscal Year ending March 31. Thus, "FY2010" refers to the last nine months of 2009 plus the first three months of 2010.

173

record in China has been very impressive. In calendar year 2008, Jaguar sales in China were only about a thousand cars, accounting for less than 2 percent of the brand's worldwide sales. In contrast, for the fiscal year ending March 31, 2013, Jaguar sold about nine thousand cars in China, accounting for over 15 percent of worldwide sales.

The data for Land Rover are equally impressive. In calendar year 2008, Land Rover sales in China were about twelve thousand vehicles, or 6 percent of worldwide sales. In contrast, for the fiscal year ending March 31, 2013, Land Rover sold sixty-eight thousand vehicles in China, accounting for over 20 percent of worldwide sales. For the fiscal year 2012–2013, JLR earned over £5.0 billion in revenues from China. These are large numbers. Success in China has played a crucial role in JLR's ability to compete worldwide, as it has given the company the scale and cash flow to invest in new technologies, new designs, new production facilities, and relentless advertising. In December 2013, JLR announced that it would expand its global production footprint by building its first plant in Brazil.

Manufacturing in China

As part of their new strategy, in 2011 JLR executives began discussions with potential Chinese partners to set up a joint venture manufacturing operation in the country. Domestic manufacturing would mean that JLR vehicles could be sold in China without having to pay a 25-percent import duty. Thus retail prices would come down by at least 20 percent, giving a significant boost to the competitiveness of these cars as well the size of the potential market for them. In March 2012, JLR announced an agreement with Chery Automobile Co., a manufacturer of passenger cars, minivans, and SUVs based in Anhui, a province in eastern China. Among the bigger domestic car companies in China, Chery was one of the few that did not have a foreign joint venture partner at that time. In November 2012, the JLR-Chery joint venture received formal approval from the National Development and Reform Commission (NDRC), China's powerful planning body. By all accounts, it appears that this may be the last domestic-foreign joint venture in the auto sector that the Chinese government would permit in the medium term. The government's industrial policy for the auto sector is now placing a much higher priority on consolidation among existing players rather than establishment of new players.

Shortly after receiving the NDRC approval in November 2012, Ratan Tata joined JLR and Chery executives to lay the cornerstone for Chery Jaguar Land Rover Automotive Company Ltd., the newly formed 50:50 joint venture. With an investment of about RMB 12 billion (US$1.9 billion), the joint venture would have the capacity to manufacture 130,000 cars and 130,000 engines per year—numbers that could rise in future years. Production was slated to start in July 2014 with initial plans to manufacture 34,000 Range Rover Evoques, 43,000 Land Rover Freelander 2s, 30,000 Jaguars, and 23,000 cars for Chery. The plant was also expected to manufacture engines for both JLR and Chery. When asked whether JLR vehicles manufactured in China would still enjoy the cachet of British brands, Bob Grace responded:

> Jaguar Land Rover customers won't be disappointed when they see the vehicles coming off the production line here in China—they will be true to the spirit of Jaguars and Land Rovers in exactly the same way they are today. In English we have an expression—the proof of the pudding is in the eating. We understand what the ingredients are, we understand how to cook, but unfortunately we have to wait.... for you to be able to see the proof of the pudding.[5]

In an October 2013 article, *Global Times*, one of the leading official newspapers of the Chinese government, also sounded optimistic about JLR's future in China:

> It is somewhat surprising that JLR—a company on the verge of bankruptcy five years ago, which was sold by Ford to India's Tata Motors—has rebounded so quickly and already reported such pretty sales numbers in China. In the first three quarters of this year, JLR recorded a total sale of 66,505 units in the Chinese market, up 18.3 percent year-on-year, a figure that was driven mainly by sales of its Land Rover SUV models. Chinese consumers were even willing to pay an extra 400,000 yuan to buy a Land Rover vehicle in China, where strong demand is currently outstripping supply. Fueled by rapid growth in the SUV sector in China, which surged over 45 percent year-on-year in the first three quarters this year, Land Rover SUVs are

expected to see even better performance after its localization in the future.[6]

China today is the world's largest auto market. Forecasts suggest that it may account for 25 percent or more of the global auto market by 2020. In light of the accomplishments to date and prospects for the future, it is hard to disagree with Bob Grace's characterization of Jaguar Land Rover China, speaking to us when we met him in January 2013: "The journey has only begun."

7

Committed Pioneers
Chinese Companies in India

India needs outside capital, and expertise in manufacturing and infrastructure. China must invest its surplus funds abroad, ideally not just in government bonds—as mostly happens in America—and ideally in countries that are not about to go belly up, as may happen in Europe. Chinese investment in India is an idea whose time has come, if only the two sides can conquer a legacy of mistrust.[1]

—"Friend, Enemy, Rival, Investor," *Economist*, June 2012

Indian businessmen and women who find China baffling and a land of mystery may want to take solace in the fact that their Chinese counterparts coming to India find that country no less baffling. Consider, for example, the following observations shared with us by the Chinese head of international business for a successful auto-parts company based in southern China. The company is a significant exporter to the Indian market but is keen to start manufacturing in India. As the Chinese yuan has appreciated significantly against the Indian rupee, Indian customers have been pressing them to manufacture in India. Given the lower labor costs in India, there also appear to be opportunities to use India, rather than China, as a manufacturing base for exports to Europe. This executive has visited India several times to figure out what to do. We interviewed him in 2012 just as he was about to embark on another trip to India.

> The central government's attitude is very positive but, in practice, the policies remain not very friendly. India is totally different from China. The economy is dominated by family-controlled private companies who have a very good relationship with the government. If they see you as a competitor, they don't want to let you come in and take any share from them.... Also, the procedures can take a very long time. The government has set up industrial parks but, if you apply for the land, it can take more than one year to get it. In China, the process is very quick. Of course, you can get privately owned land in India much more quickly but then you run the risk that the ownership may not be clean.... There's also a big difference in the attitudes of Indian versus Chinese workers.... We've concluded that we cannot run the Indian operations by bringing Chinese managers. We have to hire local people and build a team. But, it's a big challenge to figure out who the right people could be and to build trust. For Chinese private investors like us, trust is very, very important.

Notwithstanding early-stage frustrations reflected in these comments, many Chinese companies have figured out how to master the learning curve and succeed in India. Currently, 107 companies across a diversity of sectors belong to the New Delhi–based Chamber of Chinese Enterprises in India (in comparison, about 150 companies from India are registered in China). Naturally, there is significant variation in the scale and scope of these companies' activities. As with Indian companies in China, the number of Chinese companies with sizeable operations in India is still small. However, as we discussed in Chapter One, the picture is changing rapidly. We begin with an assessment of Chinese investments in India in the context of the overall trends in outward FDI from China and inbound FDI into India.

Chinese Investments into India in the Broader Context

There are no reliable data on the exact amount of FDI from China into India or from India into China. Building on discussions with officials at the embassies of the two countries in New Delhi and Beijing, our own estimate is that, at the end of 2012, the stock of Chinese FDI into India stood at about US$800 million, and the stock of Indian FDI into China at about US$500 million. Although these may appear to be small numbers, they need to be interpreted in light of the fact that outward FDI from both China and India is a very recent phenomenon. We examine here the data for China, whose outward FDI figures are significantly higher than those for India.

According to UNCTAD data, at the end of 2012, the total stock of China's outward FDI was US$509 billion; that is, 2.2 percent of the world total (in comparison, China's GDP added up to 11.3 percent of the world's GDP). About 80 percent of this stems from FDI flows after 2007. More important, the bulk of this FDI has gone into resource sectors in developing economies. The stock of FDI into the United States adds up to only US$23 billion, 4.5 percent of China's total outward FDI, and that into Europe adds up to only US$32 billion, 6.3 percent of China's total outward FDI. Even in the case of FDI into the United States and Europe, about a quarter of the investment has gone into oil, gas, and other natural resources.[2] In short, China's investments into nonresource sectors in the United States and Europe *combined* add up to only about US$40 billion.

India's economy is about one-twentieth the size of the combined economies of the United States and Europe. Thus if India had the same technological and brand strength as the United States and Europe, one would expect Chinese FDI into India to add up to US$2 billion at present. Instead, as we noted earlier, it is US$800 million—a reasonable number, given that India does not have anywhere close to the technological or brand strength of the developed economies. What India offers is a market opportunity. So far, Chinese companies have been able to capture this opportunity via exports from

China. As the scale of Indian markets becomes larger and Chinese costs escalate, Chinese companies are beginning to shift from exports to investments.

What lies ahead? Between now and 2025, we expect five key developments:

- By 2025, China's GDP is likely to be two to three times larger in real terms than it is now.
- Outward FDI from China is likely to grow faster than GDP.
- By 2025, India's economy is likely to be three times as large in real terms as it is now.
- India is becoming and will continue to become more open to foreign investments, including those from China.
- Over the next decade, Chinese investments in India are likely to grow via not just organic but also inorganic routes—that is, both directly through Chinese acquisitions in India as well as indirectly through third-country acquisitions.

As Chinese companies make acquisitions in the United States and Europe, they will increasingly find themselves owning full-fledged operations in India as well. As a mirror-image phenomenon, look at Tata Motors' multibillion-dollar revenues from China (and the one-billion-dollar manufacturing investment currently under way) as a result of the company acquiring the U.K.-based Jaguar Land Rover.

Taking all of these developments plus inflation into account, we deem it entirely possible that, by 2025, the stock of Chinese FDI into India could be US$30 billion or, if Chinese industrial clusters come to be established, even larger. This projection refers only to equity ownership of 10 percent or more in an India-based company. It does not include loans or minority stakes.

Chinese companies with significant sales, manufacturing, and/or R&D activities in India include companies in the machinery sector (such as Shanghai Electric, TBEA, and TWBB), steel products (Xinxing Heavy Machinery), telecom hardware, software and services (Huawei and ZTE), PCs and smartphones (Lenovo), consumer durables (Haier), construction equipment (Sany and Liugong), and the automotive sector (Shanghai Auto,[3] Wanfeng Aluminum Wheels, Yapp Automotive Parts). Others, such as Alibaba Group in e-commerce and Tencent in gaming and mobile internet services, are still in the very early stages. In this chapter, we review the India journeys of some of the more prominent companies and draw the lessons offered by their experiences. These lessons are relevant not just for other Chinese companies considering entry into India but also for Indian companies considering entry into China.

CHINESE POWER EQUIPMENT SUPPLIERS

The importing of power machinery from China has been one of the thorniest and most complex issues in the economic relationship between India and China. Power machinery constitutes the biggest category in Chinese exports to India, thereby also emerging as one of the biggest factors in India's growing trade deficit with its northern neighbor.

As illustrated starkly by the widespread power outage in July 2012 (which may have affected more than six hundred million people), India's electricity production remains well below the country's needs. According to World Bank data, in 2012, India generated only 0.85 mWh (megawatt hours) of electricity on a *per capita* basis, compared with 3.66 mWh for China and 3.19 mWh for the world. Not surprisingly, rapid growth in electricity production has been one of the major planks in the Indian government's plans for building up the country's infrastructure. For nearly a decade, government policies have also permitted and encouraged private companies to enter almost all segments of the power sector. The list of these so-called "independent power producers" includes some of the biggest industrial groups in the country (such as Reliance, Tata, and Adani) as well as new entrants (such as Bharat Light and Power and Kiran Energy). As a result of these moves, India's electricity production has gone up rapidly—by a whopping 32 percent during 2007–2012, relative to a 13-percent growth in worldwide electricity production during this period. However, as the low per capita figures indicate, India continues to suffer from a chronic power deficit.

185

In such a context, the independent power producers have been eager buyers of Chinese machinery from companies such as Shanghai Electric, Dongfang Electric, Harbin Electric, and TBEA. In 2010, Reliance Power signed a landmark deal with Shanghai Electric whereby it would buy over US$8 billion worth of power equipment, perhaps the largest cross-border deal ever signed in the power sector worldwide. Significantly for Reliance Power, this deal also included low-cost financing from a syndicate of some of China's largest banks. Our own interviews with senior executives at Shanghai Electric suggest that, during 2007–2012, India has been the single largest source of export revenues for the company. On an aggregated basis, Chinese vendors are reported to have captured a sizeable share of the power machinery market in India.[4]

The primary factors driving Indian power companies—especially the independent power producers—to buy from Chinese vendors have included

- A 20- to 30-percent lower price
- Significantly lower-cost financing than is available from banks in India
- Shorter delivery periods (until at least 2011)
- Selective technological limitations of domestic suppliers—for example, in the case of ultra mega power projects (UMPP) with a generating capacity of 4,000 MW and above and high-voltage transformers with a capacity greater than 400 kV

Policy making by the Indian government has been driven by a number of conflicting forces:

- The imperative to boost electricity production at a rapid rate while keeping tariffs low, an objective that favors permitting barrier-free imports from China
- Lobbying by independent power producers who are powerful and who prefer low-cost sourcing, especially when it is financed by low-cost loans
- Lobbying by domestic power machinery companies—such as Bharat Heavy Electricals Limited and Larsen & Toubro—who also are powerful, have been deeply unhappy with "unfair" competition from Chinese suppliers, and argue that Chinese suppliers have had a spotty record in the area of after-sales services
- The government's policy goal to boost India's manufacturing sector from about 15 percent of GDP to 25 percent over the next decade
- A ballooning trade deficit, which hurts GDP growth while also putting downward pressure on the value of the Indian rupee

In 2012, the arguments favoring a clampdown on imports prevailed, and the Indian government imposed a number of duties—adding up to 21 percent—on imports of power machinery into the country. However, deals that had already been signed were grandfathered in and thus exempt from these duties. As a result, these moves have yet to have any material effect on the trade pattern between India and China. It is likely, however, that as Indian power producers continue to place ever-larger orders for machinery, Chinese companies will have little choice but to shift their strategies from exporting from China to investing and manufacturing in India. In 2012, Shanghai Electric's top leaders indicated that they were leaning in this direction. To date, however, they have not made any manufacturing investments in India.

There are some exceptions, such as the Tebian Electrical Apparatus Stock Company (TBEA). TBEA is China's largest company in the power transmission equipment and related products and services industry. The company's core business is power transformers; it is regarded as particularly strong in the high-voltage segment. High-voltage transformers play a key role in the transmission of electricity over long distances. As India's power generation capacity ramps up at a faster-than-GDP growth rate, the demand for high-voltage transformers is expected to increase even more rapidly.

In recent years, India has been one of the most attractive markets for TBEA's exports from China. However, two new realities are pushing TBEA to begin switching its strategy from exports to domestic production in India. First, as the Indian transformer market grows, domestic production in India offers better prospects for capturing economies of scale. Second, as noted earlier, the Indian government is increasingly unwilling to accept the growing trade imbalance with China. Regulatory barriers to imports of Chinese power equipment give an advantage to other players, such as Siemens and ABB, which have full-fledged subsidiaries in India that also happen to be listed on the Bombay Stock Exchange.

In 2009, TBEA began discussions with Bharat Heavy Electricals Limited (BHEL), a public sector enterprise, to explore the idea of setting up a joint venture in India. At that time, BHEL's transformer capabilities went up to only about 400 kV. In contrast, TBEA had the technology to manufacture electric power transformers of up to 1,000 kV. TBEA liked the idea of partnering with a government-owned entity in India. For its part, BHEL viewed a joint venture with TBEA as an effective strategy to fend off the challenge from Western giants. As one analyst with a brokerage house in India noted, "BHEL does not have the technology for high-voltage transformers and equipment. Any such collaboration will help BHEL as it will be able to bid for high-voltage orders such as those of PowerGrid."[5]

As it transpired, TBEA and BHEL were unable to agree on the terms for setting up a JV. In May 2011, TBEA's top leadership indicated their interest in setting up a wholly owned manufacturing facility near Vadodara in the state of Gujarat. They were attracted by the Gujarat government's reputation for being investor-friendly, as well as by the fact that Narendra Modi, the chief minister of Gujarat, appeared interested in developing the Central Gujarat region as an energy equipment manufacturing hub for the country's power sector.[6] In November 2011, the two sides signed a memorandum of understanding, according to which TBEA would invest 2,500 crore rupees (about US$500 million) to set up a TBEA Green Energy Park in the state. In the first phase, to be started immediately on signing, TBEA would invest 400 crore rupees (about US$80 million) to build an ultra-high-voltage transformer plant. In turn, the government of Gujarat offered all possible help in the provisioning of necessary infrastructure as well as various financial incentives available under the policies of the state and central governments.

By early 2013, the TBEA Green Energy Park was in operation and manufacturing transformers up to 756 kV. Gopal Krishan Gupta, CEO, TBEA Energy (India), seemed optimistic about the prospects: "The power transmission and distribution system goes through distinct stages of development. The natural progression is from isolated small grids operating at low voltage to regional grids operating at high voltages. As the power consumption increases, there is need to transfer large amounts of power from generators to consumers. In India, there will be a significant growth in the T&D systems as per capita power consumption increases to global levels."[7] In an interesting new development, TBEA has found itself competing in India not only with the Indian and Western players but also with Baoding Tianwei Baodian Electric Co. (TWBB), its biggest Chinese competitor. In May 2012, TWBB incorporated a majority-owned joint venture with Gujarat-based Atlanta Electricals Private Limited to also manufacture high-voltage transformers in India. This joint venture is located not far from the TBEA Green Energy Park. As Jiao Zihe, director of the TWBB-Atlanta joint venture, observed: "Yes, we are competitors not only in China but also at the global level. In China's transmission sector, we [TBEA and TWBB] are the biggest players.... The presence of a lot of suppliers will be good for the overall development of the sector and benefit consumers in India."[8]

XINDIA STEELS: A PROMISING JOINT VENTURE IN THE STEEL SECTOR

Xindia Steels Limited is one of the largest India-based joint ventures between Chinese and Indian companies. This is the first Chinese investment in the Indian steel industry. Xindia Steels currently produces iron ore pellets, which are used as feedstock in blast furnaces and direct-reduced iron plants, and the company has plans to produce ductile iron (DI) pipes[9] and other steel products. The company's primary offices are in Bangalore and the production facilities are located in the Koppal District of Karnataka.

Xindia Steels was set up in January 2008, when the joint venture partners signed the contract during Prime Minister Manmohan Singh's visit to China. Initially there were four partners, two from China (Xinxing Heavy Machinery Limited and China Minmetals Corporation) and two from India (Kelachandra Group and Manasara Group) (see "Profile of Original JV Partners in Xindia Steel"). The Chinese partners held the majority stake of 55 percent; the Indian partners owned the rest. By 2011, three more investors had joined as minority equity holders in Xindia Steel—McWane Inc. (a U.S.-based company and the world's largest producer of DI pipes), Shanxi Hongda Iron and Steel Group (from China), and the Joinus Venture Capital Company (also from China).

Profile of Original JV Partners in Xindia Steel

Xinxing Heavy Machinery is a member of the Xinxing Cathay International Group, a state-owned enterprise and one of China's one hundred largest companies. Xinxing is a diversified corporation, with businesses in several sectors. Its core product lines include DI pipes, where it is one of the world's two largest manufacturers and commands a 45-percent market share in China. Xinxing also exports DI pipes to over one hundred countries.

China Minmetals Corporation is also one of China's largest state-owned enterprises. Its core businesses include exploration, mining, smelting, processing, and trading of metals and minerals. Minmetals has enjoyed over thirty years of trade relations with India, which is one of its biggest trading partners. Minmetals imports iron ore from India into China and exports coal from China to India.

Kelachandra Group is an India-based diversified business group with interests in real estate, apparel, hospitality, travel, and agricultural commodities such as spices, coffee, and rubber.

Manasara Group is an India-based diversified business group with investments in telecom, software, steel, and infrastructure companies.

The JV partners' business logic has been very clear: leverage the technology, project management skills, and best practices of the Chinese and American partners to become one of India's lowest-cost producers of iron and steel finished products, especially pipes. The demand for steel products in India was expected to grow dramatically. In 2008, steel consumption per capita was only 43.2 kilograms in India, compared with 195.1 kilograms worldwide and 336.4 kilograms in China.[10] The Indian government was keen to ensure that the anticipated rapid growth in demand be met by domestic production rather than imports. The partners contributed complementary strengths—technology, global reach, local relationships, ownership of iron ore resources, land rights, and so forth. The founders also expected that the JV might eventually be able to leverage the partners' global distribution network to export pipes from India.

By August 2011, Xindia Steels had completed the first phase of the partners' plans for the JV. At a total investment of over 250 crore rupees (about US$50 million), this phase included facilities to manufacture 0.8 million tons per annum of iron ore pellets. The Chinese partners' initial preference had been to bring in a Chinese contractor to build the pelletization plant. However, after some back-and-forth discussions, they conceded to demands from the state government that Xindia use a local rather than a Chinese contractor. Although these discussions caused some delay in the start of construction, the final agreement to use an Indian contractor prevented the project from going off track. It is also noteworthy that the State Bank of India became one of the three banks that provided loans to Xindia. This was the first time that an Indian bank had provided loans to a Chinese majority-held company.

In his speech at the commissioning of this plant, Mr. Zhang Yan, China's ambassador to India, made some highly pertinent observations:

> Xindia Steels Limited is the first of its kind joint venture between China and India in the field of iron and steel industry—a crucial sector for economic development of any country. As a fast growing economy, India has enjoyed a growth of 8 to 9 per cent annually in recent years. Against this backdrop, the demand for iron and steel and their products by the Indian market is rising steadily. Therefore, the Xindia Steel Limited project is very timely. The whole project will be implemented in a phased manner....

> It is also important to note that, apart from turning out iron and steel products, Xindia will also create job opportunities for the local people. We are glad to see that Xindia has already provided around 200 jobs after [completing] the first phase. According to the projection, Xindia would create more than 10,000 direct job opportunities after [completion of] the third phase....

> It is my view that China and India should make new efforts to diversify our economic cooperation by expanding the scope of cooperation. I am happy to see that, while maintaining the strong momentum in trade, both sides start to look for new cooperation in mutual investment. It is the Chinese government's policy to encourage technically and financially capable companies to "go abroad" and invest overseas or establish joint ventures with companies from India and other countries. We also welcome Indian companies to invest in

China. I hope the commissioning of this project will herald a new wave of cooperation in mutual investment between China and India.[11]

Over the following year and a half, Xindia Steel also completed Phase II, which included setting up a blast furnace with a pipe plant to manufacture ductile iron pipes and pig iron, a key raw material for steel plants and foundries. In early 2013, the company was in the early stages of implementing Phase III and was conducting environmental impact studies for a 1.2-million-ton integrated steel plant along with a 160 MW power plant. Subsequently, the JV partners planned to increase the steel production capacity to five million tons and the pellet plant capacity to six million tons. The total investment across all of these phases was projected to exceed 8,500 crore rupees (over US$1.5 billion).

HUAWEI'S MULTIDIMENSIONAL ENGAGEMENT WITH INDIA

A global giant in telecom equipment and services, Huawei is China's largest and most admired technology company. Headquartered in the southern Chinese city of Shenzhen, it reported 2012 revenues of US$35.3 billion, derived one-third from China and two-thirds from foreign markets. Huawei's core business—and the source of 73 percent of 2012 revenues—is network equipment and services for telecom carriers. The rest comes from communications equipment and services for enterprises (other than telecom carriers) and consumers. In the market for carriers, Huawei is now the second largest company in the world, after Ericsson. Other major competitors include, in the carrier market, Nokia, Alcatel-Lucent, and the Chinese company ZTE; in the enterprise market, Cisco and Juniper Networks; and in the consumer devices market, companies such as Samsung, Apple, and Lenovo.

Huawei was founded in 1987 by Ren Zhengfei, a former officer in the engineering corps of the People's Liberation Army. He started the company by selling telecom equipment imported from Hong Kong. Five years later, he transformed Huawei into a product company by making a digital telephone switch with greater capacity than any other competitor in China. The rest, as the saying goes, is history. Huawei grew rapidly, riding the explosive telecom-infrastructure boom in China.

Our own analysis of Huawei's evolution suggests that the company's growth is a result of several key factors: entrepreneurial determination, excellence in management, and significant help from the Chinese government. Reflecting his military background, Ren Zhengfei has instilled a wolf-like culture in the company. He has urged his employees to learn from wolves, who have a keen sense of smell, are aggressive, and hunt in packs. In particular, he has pushed Huawei's marketing arm to cultivate a high degree of aggressiveness.[12] Ren Zhengfei knows, however, that entrepreneurial ambition cannot by itself create a large and successful enterprise. Thus early in the company's history he started to study and replicate the world's best systems and processes, and he has sought extensive consulting help from the likes of IBM, Hay Group, Towers Perrin, and PriceWaterhouseCoopers.

Ren has also been driven in the quest to make Huawei a technology powerhouse. In 2012, Huawei reported that it spent a hefty 13.7 percent of revenues on R&D. The company's leaders have long claimed that more than 40 percent of Huawei's total staff is employed in the R&D function. Huawei has also been one of the largest filers of patent applications in the world. Many in the industry believe that, although Huawei is now quite careful about honoring others' intellectual property rights, this was not always the case. In 2004, Cisco filed a lawsuit against Huawei that was later settled out of court by the two companies.[13] In early 2013, Cisco reportedly introduced a new policy whereby it will no longer hire any former Huawei employee in India unless he or she has spent at least three years with other companies after leaving Huawei.[14] In terms of government help, Huawei has long been regarded as a national champion by the Chinese government. As a result, it has enjoyed preferred access to telecom carriers in China, all of which are state-owned enterprises. Huawei also acknowledges that for several years it has enjoyed a low-cost credit line from state-owned Chinese banks of up to US$30 billion to support its export financing.[15]

Huawei's India strategy has been explicitly multidimensional from day one—viewing India as a global hub for technical talent in R&D and operations support, as one of the world's largest and fastest-growing markets for telecom equipment, and as a possible base for manufacturing. Huawei entered India in 1999 by setting up a software R&D center in Bangalore, several years before it got its first order from an Indian telecom carrier. In 2003, this R&D center received the prestigious CMM-Level 5 certification for leading-edge competence in software development. This was the first time that any unit of Huawei had received this award.

Over time, the R&D center has grown in both size and importance. At present, it is staffed by over two thousand software engineers and is Huawei's largest R&D center outside China. According to the company, the center develops components, platforms, and products in areas such as next generation networks, network management, data communication, optical transmission, and mobile handset applications.

In addition to the R&D center in Bangalore, Huawei has leveraged Indian talent in other areas as well. In 2012, the company established a number of other centers in Bangalore, all with *global* charters:

- A Global Solutions Service Center (GSS) aimed at providing presales technical support and designing customized solutions for the company's offshore clients
- A Global Service Resource Center (GSRC) aimed at providing after-sales technical support and delivery solutions to clients around the world
- A Global Network Operations Center (GNOC) aimed at providing a range of professional services including network design, customer support, network optimization, systems integration, and network transformation—all as part of Huawei's global managed services platform

Huawei is also in the process of setting up a Global Technology Center (GTEC) in Bangalore. According to Cai Liqun,

CEO, Huawei India, "We have GTECs in China, but this will be the first outside China. Indians have advantages in both language and technology. That is what we want to capitalise on through this centre."[16]

In terms of capturing the market opportunities in India, Huawei's progress has been driven by a number of factors, including market dynamics, the scope of the company's product and service offerings, and the Indian government's on-again-off-again security concerns with Huawei's equipment. When Huawei entered India in 1999 to set up an R&D center, it was a largely unknown vendor with little credibility. Over time, however, the company's tenacity and determination began to yield results. Huawei received its first orders from smaller operators such as Uninor and Sistema Shyam Teleservices. It then moved up to signing orders with mid-sized operators such as BSNL and Tata Teleservices. More recently, the company has started securing orders from the largest Indian carriers such as Bharti Airtel and Reliance. It has also started supplying equipment and services to Bharti Airtel's operations outside India, such as those in Bangladesh and Africa.

Huawei earned an estimated US$1.2 billion in revenues from the Indian market in 2012. Industry analysts estimate the company's share of the Indian market to be as follows: 26 percent in wireless infrastructure (third position after Ericsson and Nokia), 18 percent in transmission equipment (third position after Alcatel-Lucent and ECI), 17 percent in managed services (third position after Nokia and Ericsson), 18 percent in wireless broadband (second position after ZTE), and a market-leading 55 percent share in data cards (followed by ZTE in the second position with a 32 percent share).[17] During the period 2011–2013, Huawei, like all other telecom vendors, has suffered from a slowdown in telecom investments in India due to a combination of factors including regulatory uncertainty, corruption allegations against certain telecom carriers, and cutthroat competition that keeps margins narrow and reduces carriers' cash flows.

Looking ahead, the prospects look considerably brighter. As the government gives out new licenses for 3G and 4G spectrums, carriers are expected to start investing again. More important, these faster and higher-capacity transmission technologies are more capital intensive than older ones. Huawei, in particular, also expects to benefit from an expansion in its own scope of products and services. It is now aggressively pursuing business from enterprise customers (other than telecom carriers) as well as consumers (via smartphones).

It is worth noting that Huawei's ability to sell to telecom carriers in India has long been dogged by the Indian government's concerns that its hardware and/or software may contain pathways that could allow the Chinese government to engage in spying or, in the event of a conflict, cyber-warfare. In its defense, Huawei has consistently argued that it is a reliable and trustworthy vendor and that it remains ready to work with the Indian government to set up appropriate mechanisms to ensure that its equipment can be regarded as secure.

On the manufacturing front, Huawei does have a small unit that produces fiber-optic equipment near Chennai. However, the bulk of the company's equipment is imported from China, where it is assembled by global subcontractors such as Flextronics. The Indian government is not happy about this. In 2013, the Department of Telecommunications (DoT) excluded both Huawei and ZTE from its master list of domestic manufacturers. Under the new regulations set forth by DoT, mobile carriers would be required to increase their purchases from domestic manufacturers in a phased manner, with the goal that 80 percent of all sourcing would be from local suppliers by 2020. As of this writing, the fate of these regulations remains unclear, as they affect not just Chinese vendors but also those from other countries. The U.S. government is putting enormous pressure on the Indian government to not adopt preferential market access norms. For its part, Huawei has indicated that, as sales volumes in India go up, it would start increasing its manufacturing footprint in India.

Huawei has also taken other steps to make itself a welcome player in India. Many of the company's India-based Chinese executives have adopted Indian first names. As a case in point, when we met Yao Weimin, vice-president of corporate affairs at Huawei India, he shared a business card imprinted with the name "Rajiv Yao." In 2013, Huawei also announced that it will start offering "phantom shares" to the top 20 percent of its six-thousand-strong workforce in India—making it the first country outside China to implement this new policy. According to Cai Liqun, Huawei India's CEO, "Phantom shares are similar to ESOPs, and employees are eligible to a dividend every year, enabling them to share the company's profits. The top 20 percent of our workforce here will be eligible for fresh shares every year."[18] Our own discussions with Huawei senior executives suggest that they remain committed to India as an important global market, a source of top talent, and a target for investment.

LENOVO'S DETERMINED PUSH TO BECOME THE MARKET LEADER IN INDIA

Lenovo entered India with a bang in 2005 when it purchased the worldwide PC business of IBM Corporation. Prior to this acquisition, the company was focused largely on the domestic Chinese market, where it was the dominant market leader with a share of about 35 percent. With revenues of over US$3 billion in 2004, Lenovo ranked eighth among PC companies globally. Its acquisition of IBM's PC business catapulted it into the number three position, after Hewlett-Packard (HP) and Dell. The acquisition also gave Lenovo ownership of the "Think" brand and the right to use the IBM brand for a period of five years.

The acquisition brought together two businesses with very different strengths. The IBM PC business was aimed primarily at the B2B market, with 75 percent of revenues coming from large enterprises and the rest from small and medium businesses (SMB). Further, IBM was not particularly strong in China's PC market. In contrast, Lenovo was dominant in China but almost nonexistent elsewhere. Also, Lenovo derived the bulk of its revenues from the B2C market, and its distribution system for PCs was far more extensive than any other computer company's.

Right from the get-go, Lenovo's top leaders viewed India as mission critical in their ambition to capture the number one position in the PC business globally. Although PC penetration in India was well behind that in China, the market's growth rate and potential size meant that, over time, India could become almost as important to Lenovo as China. Also, many of the factors that accounted for Lenovo's success in China could potentially be replicated in India. Consistent with these beliefs, one of their early moves was to elevate India to the level of a separate geographical market alongside the Americas, EMEA (Europe, Middle East, and Africa), Asia Pacific, and China. They also created a dedicated advisory board for India reporting directly to chairman Yang Yuanqing.

Post-acquisition, Lenovo started out in India with a 9-percent share of the overall PC market, which gave it a number three position after HP (with a 19-percent market share) and HCL (with a 13-percent market share). Lenovo also acquired IBM's manufacturing facility for assembling PCs in Pondicherry. The key planks in the company's strategy to grow market share were to focus on the consumer and SMB segments; to expand the sales and distribution network, especially in Tier 2 and 3 cities; and to invest in brand visibility and recall by placing ads across all media—print, radio, television, and the Internet. As part of this strategy, the company started placing the Lenovo brand in Bollywood films as well as popular television programs such as *Kaun Banega Crorepati* (featured in the Hollywood film *Slumdog Millionaire*). Lenovo also entered into tie-ins with leading telecom operators for bundling PCs with fixed broadband connections and/or wireless data cards (similar to the practice being adopted by HP and HCL). The company also opened an Innovation Centre in Mumbai aimed at solving enterprise customers' hardware and software problems—Lenovo's third such center in the world after those in the United States and China. Lenovo also established a global marketing hub in Bangalore, responsible for all marketing communications worldwide outside of China. This hub would serve over fifty countries and drive core marketing functions such as market research, strategic marketing services, analytics, and ROI measurement.

During 2006–2008, as part of its strategy to establish an extensive distribution network, the company continued channel expansion across 450 cities through Lenovo Exclusive Outlets (LES) as well as multibrand retail stores. It also started opening scaled-down versions of the exclusive stores, called LES Lite, in smaller cities. Lenovo's managers considered exclusive stores as critical to building the company's brand image, cultivating brand loyalty, and ensuring repeat sales: "One of our main areas of focus is to increase the depth of our penetration in the tier-II and tier-III cities in India. Improving our supply chain efficiencies and helping our business partners do excellent business amidst tough economic conditions will be our focus areas as well. We are sure of achieving these, if we get closer to our customers and partner ecosystem, listen to their pain points, and address them effectively. A closer collaboration process forms our agenda this year."[19]

Notwithstanding these moves, 2008 and 2009 turned out to be challenging years for Lenovo—globally as well as in India. As a result of the global recession, the enterprise market—the core strength of the company outside China—went into a slump. This development hurt Lenovo more than it hurt other companies. The board asked CEO William Amelio, an American, to step down. Liu Chuanzhi, the company's founder, returned as chairman, and Yang Yuanqing gave up the chairman's role to take charge as the new CEO. During this period, Lenovo's performance in India also gave no cause for celebration. Its competitors, especially Dell, played an exceptionally aggressive game, and Lenovo ended 2009 with a market share below 5 percent.

The company also suffered from an embarrassing incident in early 2009 when it was discovered that the ten thousand computers it had just distributed to India's Income Tax Department had been installed with a wallpaper showing territory claimed by India to be part of China—a criminal offense in India! Although the computers had been manufactured at Lenovo's Indian factory, the software came from the company's U.S. operations. Lenovo was quick to admit its error and worked expeditiously with the Income Tax Department to delete the offending maps. Fortunately for the company, the media portrayed this incident as the result of negligence rather than malicious intentions. Nonetheless, it was not a positive development in what was already proving to be an exceptionally tough year for Lenovo.

The new leadership of Liu Chuanzhi and Yang Yuanqing set a clear goal to make Lenovo the world's market share leader in PCs. They devised a new global strategy—*protect and attack*—aimed at protecting the core markets (China and the enterprise business inherited from IBM) while attacking higher-growth segments such as consumers, SMB, and emerging markets. In these "attack" markets, the strategic priority would be volume rather than profits. They also sharpened the company's branding strategy. The Lenovo Thinkpad (with an emphasis on the "Thinkpad" element of the brand) would be positioned as classy and dependable. In contrast, the Lenovo Ideapad (with an emphasis on the "Lenovo" element of the brand) would be positioned as a fun device.

By the fourth quarter of 2009, Lenovo's market share in India had recovered to 8.1 percent. In 2010, the company sent Alex Li, a Chinese manager, to take over as the new VP, Transactions Segment, Lenovo India. Li's mission was to accelerate replication of the company's China model in India. The key elements of this model were a lean but ubiquitous distribution network, a high degree of visibility into the entire sales and distribution system, and a high degree of attention to customers. Li moved rapidly to reengineer the distribution system. He consolidated the nine national distributors into four and also established new policies for channel management. Regional distributors now would have to purchase from just one designated national distributor so that the company could keep better track of sales and inventory. Previously, many regional distributors would buy from a different national distributor each time, thereby taking on too much debt and also reducing Lenovo's visibility into actual sales. Further, Lenovo Exclusive Stores would now be prohibited from selling PCs in bulk. They were to sell only to consumers and SMBs and to devote greater personalized attention to them.

In 2011, Lenovo opened the four-hundredth LES Lite store in India. Amar Babu, managing director of Lenovo India, commented: "With PC penetration still in single digits in most parts of India, there is a huge opportunity for us to drive industry growth in India's hinterland. We expect a significant increase in PC purchases from consumers in tiers 3 to 5 cities and towns and are focusing on retail penetration as a key growth driver. This 400th LES Lite is a significant milestone in our ambitious retail expansion, which is in sync with our overall retail strategy to have 1000 Lenovo exclusive outlets across India by March 2012."[20] By the second quarter of 2011, Lenovo's market share in India had recovered to about 10 percent. Later that year, the company also launched tablet computers in the Indian market.

The new strategy—protect and attack—proved to be a success not just in India but globally. Lenovo ended 2011 as the world's number two PC vendor by market share, behind HP but ahead of Dell. Emerging markets played a major role in this trajectory, with Lenovo's sales growing two to three times faster than sales of the industry as a whole.

In India, as elsewhere, Lenovo continued its vigorous pursuit of the consumer and SMB segments. The company opened its one-thousandth dedicated Lenovo store in 2012. The triumphal moment, however, arrived at the end of the first quarter of 2012, when Lenovo overtook Dell to become the top PC seller in India, with a market share of about 16 percent. The company achieved this goal in part by supplying 360,000 laptops to the Tamil Nadu government at the rock-bottom price of about US$280 per unit. Lenovo, HCL, and Acer were the winners of a tender to sell nine hundred thousand laptops to the Tamil Nadu government, which planned to give these away to high school children as part of an election promise. According to Adwaita Govind Menon, head of new products at IDC

India, a market research firm, "Everyone is making a loss in the Tamil Nadu deal."[21] Dell and HP stayed away from this contract.

The year 2012 also saw India's PC industry affected severely by a steep depreciation in the Indian rupee vis-à-vis the U.S. dollar, as 90 percent of the components were imported into India and were priced in U.S. dollars. Nonetheless, the industry's growth prospects remained robust as PC penetration in India was still quite low—about 7 percent. Lenovo, HP, Acer, and Dell were now the top four competitors in India's PC market, each with a market share in the 13- to 17-percent range. The year also saw rumors that Lenovo may have been in discussions to acquire a controlling stake in India's HCL Infosystems, a move that did not materialize.

Lenovo Group ended 2012 as the world's number one PC vendor and also the market share leader in five of the seven top PC markets (China, Japan, India, Germany and Russia). Toward the end of 2012, Lenovo Group also picked India as the second country after China for the launch of the company's smartphones. This launch was very much a part of rolling out the company's global "four-screen" strategy (smartphones, smart TVs, tablets, and PCs) into India. Although there are nine hundred million cell-phone numbers in India, the number of smartphones was still only eighteen million. Given the scale of India's market, obtaining leadership in smartphones in India had the potential to play a major role in Lenovo's ability to emerge as one of the top smartphone vendors globally. It seemed clear, however, that achieving leadership in India's smartphone market would require winning a tough battle with

Samsung, which already commanded a 50-percent share of the country's market.

In February 2013, Lenovo Group held its first board meeting in India. In an interview with the *Economic Times*, chairman and CEO Yang Yuanqing shared his views regarding Lenovo's global success and India's importance to the company:

> Our success is a combination of four things: first is right strategy and good execution. The second is innovative products and third is efficiency of our delivery. And finally the diversified global leadership team which understands the needs of different geographies. On top of that, in the last four years we have had a strategy of "protect and attack." We protect our strength in our core geography and business, that is, China business and global enterprise business. And we attack new markets with new products—like emerging markets.... We want to win in India. That's the biggest initiative [for this year].[22]

Notwithstanding Lenovo's success to date, the competitive battle was far from over. Hewlett-Packard came roaring back in 2013. Under Meg Whitman, who took over as the global CEO in 2011, HP merged its printer and PC divisions into an integrated Printing and Personal Systems Group. This integration allowed HP to merge the sales and distribution channels of the two product lines into one. The company's PC business could now leverage the worldwide dominance of HP's printer business, including in India. Under Whitman, the PC business also decided to compete not only on product innovation but also on pricing. In February 2013, HP beat Lenovo to win a contract to supply 1.5 million PCs to the government of the state of Uttar Pradesh. By the second quarter of 2013, HP had surged well ahead of Lenovo in India.[23] In the battle between these two companies (and others including Dell and Acer), HP seemed to betting on the synergy between printers and PCs, whereas Lenovo seemed to put its weight behind the synergy between smartphones and PCs. Because the battle among Lenovo, HP, and Dell is a very close one in India as well as globally, the outcome is very difficult to predict.

HAIER'S ATTEMPT TO MAKE UP FOR ITS LATE START IN INDIA

With consolidated revenues of US$25.8 billion in 2012, Haier Group is the world's largest white goods manufacturer. It is also one of China's iconic and most global companies.

As with Ratan Tata at Tata Sons and N.R. Narayana Murthy at Infosys, it is impossible to separate the name of Zhang Ruimin from Haier's evolution over the last three decades. In 1984, Zhang was appointed as the general manager of Qingdao General Refrigerator Factory, a near-bankrupt company in northeastern China. The company suffered from almost every problem imaginable—workers who failed to show up, shoddy product quality, financial troubles, and very high management turnover. Among his first acts, Zhang asked the workers to take out the seventy-six malfunctioning refrigerators in inventory and destroy each and every one of them with sledgehammers. He then said, "If I allow these refrigerators to be sold today, I'm allowing them to produce more of the same faulty refrigerators. Today it's 76, tomorrow it can be 760 or even 7600."[24]

Once Zhang had turned around Qingdao Refrigerator, he went on an acquisition spree in China. By 1992, Haier Group— as the company was now called—had become the largest, most profitable, and most diversified white goods manufacturer in China. The company was famous for being the industry's undisputed leader in product quality, market-driven innovation, logistics, and after-sales service. Haier began global expansion in the early 1990s as a contract manufacturer for multinational brands in Germany, France, and the U.K. By 1999, foreign sales accounted for about 3 percent of the group's total sales. That year, the company set up an Overseas Promotion Division with the goal of more aggressive global expansion through both exports from China and local production. Unlike other Chinese companies that focused primarily on developing markets, Haier chose a totally contrarian strategy of giving primacy to developed markets such as the United States and Europe. As Zhang Ruimin, Haier's CEO, explained: "When Chinese companies expand abroad, many of them choose to first enter developing countries and later more affluent markets. But, Haier's strategy is exactly the opposite. We first get into high-end markets in the United States and Europe because we believe those markets are more mature and competition is more fierce. If we place ourselves in such situations, we can quickly spot our own problems."[25]

This strategy had been successful in some ways, but it also had a significant downside. In the developed markets such as the United States and Europe, Haier found it hard to dislodge entrenched competitors such as GE, Whirlpool, and Bosch. As a result, the company was unable to get much traction outside niche segments such as compact refrigerators and wine coolers. At the same time, this focus on developed markets delayed Haier's entry into major emerging markets such as India, Brazil, and Russia. Thus Haier had relatively small market shares in virtually all large countries outside China. As of 2010, 72.5 percent of the group's total revenues came from domestic sales in China, 14 percent from exports from China, and 13.5 percent from local production in foreign markets.[26]

Haier's foray into the Indian market began in 1999 when it set up a joint venture with Hotline, a Kolkata-based company. The new JV, Hotline Haier Alliances Ltd.—owned 70 percent by Hotline and 30 percent by Haier—ran into trouble almost as soon as it was set up. The two partners differed profoundly over the strategy to be followed. Three years later, in 2002, Haier launched a second attempt to enter India by commencing discussions with a number of Indian companies that would enable the latter to import Haier products and also provide after-sale services. Media reports quoted a Haier executive as stating that "initially, we will not set up any manufacturing in India and the partner here will have to import it, but if the market improves, we may go in for a manufacturing facility under joint venture."[27]

By 2003, however, Haier management had concluded that they would go it alone and set up Haier India as a wholly owned subsidiary. In January 2004, the company started importing white goods from China and, later in the year, also from

Thailand to take advantage of a recently signed free trade agreement between India and Thailand. Haier also signed sourcing agreements with Whirlpool India (for refrigerators) and the Indian company Voltas (for air conditioners), under which these companies would manufacture appliances for the Chinese company. The stated goal was that Haier would commence its own manufacturing in India once the sales volumes became larger. The company's top team in India consisted of three key managers—the president and CEO of Haier India and two marketing vice-presidents, one for appliances and the other for consumer electronics such as TV sets and mobile handsets. All three executives were Indian, poached from other companies in the country. Their goals for Haier in India were truly ambitious: to own 20 percent of India's white goods market and become one of the top three players in the country within five years. Should they succeed in achieving these goals, Haier India would be second only to China in terms of its revenue contribution to the company's global sales. The market penetration for consumer durables in India was still very low—about 20 percent for color televisions, about 16 percent for refrigerators, and even lower for other products such as washing machines and dishwashers.

At the time of Haier's entry into India, the market was dominated by Korean and Indian brands. Both LG and Samsung had entered the Indian market in the 1990s but with different strategies in terms of brand positioning. LG targeted the middle and low income segments, whereas Samsung targeted the high and middle income segments. LG was the clear market share leader in almost every segment—24 percent share in color televisions, 33 percent in washing machines, 26 percent in refrigerators, and 35 percent in air conditioners. Whirlpool competed closely with Samsung for the number two position. The Indian players competed largely at lower price points. At the other extreme, the Japanese companies pursued a niche premium strategy and had relatively small market shares.

LG Electronics was especially aggressive in its commitment to the Indian market. The company set up a wholly owned subsidiary in 1997. In the first year of its existence, the company decided to set up a large manufacturing plant in Greater Noida, near New Delhi. The plant would be used not only for domestic sales in India but also as a global export hub, similar to the company's export hubs in South Korea and China. LG also positioned itself as the market leader in India in terms of customizing its appliances to the unique characteristics of the Indian market. Examples include launching a TV set with a built-in cricket video game to serve the desires of millions of India's cricket fans, incorporating technology in the TV sets so that the picture brightness and contrast adjusts automatically based on the ambient lighting, incorporating an air filtration system in the air conditioners to filter out the high levels of particulate pollution in India's metropolitan cities, and equipping all appliances for the Indian market with circuits that can deal with dramatic voltage fluctuations common in the country. Over time, LG also built up the most extensive distribution, sales, and service network among all white goods competitors in India.

For a Chinese company, Haier chose an unconventional market strategy for its products in India. Haier would be positioned as a global brand and promoted as a technology leader. Consistent with this strategy, Haier products would be sold at a premium to competitors' prices. In one respect, this strategy was successful. A survey revealed that, five months after launch, 97 percent of customers thought that Haier was a German or U.S. rather than a Chinese brand. During 2005, the first full year of its operations in India, Haier recorded sales of 225 crores rupees (US$51 million), mostly from color TV sets.

In mid-2006, Haier seemed to change course and announced that it would start focusing on rural India (the bottom-of-the-pyramid market) and develop a range of India-specific products. T. K. Banerjee, Haier's India CEO at the time, noted:

Our core offerings till now have been high-end products but '07 will see us enter the mass market with direct cool refrigerators and other mass volume categories in an attempt to gain a bigger chunk of the market. This would also create equity for the brand. We entered the Indian market with a premium line of products, which prohibited our brand from building mass appeal. Although there are so many players in the market, there is enough space for players like us, [given that] the economy [is growing] at around 8–10 percent. We have a strategy in place to topple the apple cart. We are also looking at tier 2 cities with a population of over 1 lakh [100,000] as a growth potential zone so we would sell our mass market products there. With the introduction of these mass market products, the chances of the company starting manufacturing here look very likely as sourcing these low-end products would become feasible. But, it all depends on the response we get for the new range of products.[28]

In mid-2007, Haier signed a deal to acquire a manufacturing facility in Pune from Anchor Daiwoo, an almost defunct joint venture between India's Anchor Group and the troubled Korean company Daiwoo. This became Haier's first company-owned manufacturing facility in India. Spread over forty acres, the plant had enough capacity to produce refrigerators, televisions, and washing machines. Haier's initial plans were to manufacture refrigerators only and continue sourcing other products such as washing machines and air conditioners from third-party vendors. Haier also announced that it would upgrade the Pune facility to create an R&D unit for refrigerators and may explore using this facility as a base for exports to Africa, the Middle East, and neighboring countries such as Pakistan and Sri Lanka.

Despite these moves and a growing Indian market, Haier failed to make much progress during the period from 2005 to 2009. Sales in 2009 were 390 crore rupees (US$81 million), somewhat higher than in 2005, but the company was far from realizing its goal to capture a 20-percent market share and the number three position in India's white goods market. In order to redress the situation, Haier's leaders in China appointed Erica Braganza, another Indian, as the new CEO.

Braganza shifted the company's focus back to the medium and high end. As he noted in a January 2011 interview:

> As far as brand positioning is concerned, we have shifted our focus from the low end segment products to the mid to high end segment and are in the process of introducing a larger range of world class products in India. We feel Indian consumers want value for money and are ready to spend on that

experience. I believe the timing is ripe to introduce high end products in the market. We are expecting 40 percent of our turnover to come from high end products.[29]

Braganza also expanded the company's product range and the distribution network aggressively. By 2011, Haier was selling commercial freezers, commercial and consumer air conditioners, refrigerators, minibars, washing machines, and water heaters. It was also planning to offer dishwashers, laptops, home theater systems, cameras, microwave ovens, and small appliances such as blenders, juicers, teakettles, and toasters.

Sales grew quickly from 390 crore rupees (US$81 million) in 2009 to 825 crore rupees (US$180 million) in 2010, 972 crore rupees (US$207 million) in 2011, and 1203 crore rupees (US$225 million) in 2012. Refrigerators accounted for 35 percent of 2012 revenues, air conditioners for 14 percent, consumer electronics for 30 percent, and other products for the remaining 21 percent. However, Haier's market share was still relatively small—6 percent in refrigerators, 3 percent in air conditioners, and 4–5 percent in washing machines. During 2012–2013, the company also found itself facing the challenge of a steep depreciation in the Indian rupee. From January 1, 2012 to June 30, 2013, the rupee depreciated by 11 percent against the U.S. dollar and, given the Chinese yuan's appreciation vis-à-vis the dollar, an even steeper 13 percent against the yuan. This was proving to be a bigger challenge for Haier (which sourced more of its products and components from China) than it was for the Korean or Indian competitors (which relied more on manufacturing in India).

LESSONS FROM CHINESE COMPANIES' JOURNEYS IN INDIA

We summarize here the key lessons that emerge from Chinese companies' journeys into India. These lessons have relevance not only for other Chinese companies but also for Indian companies, which often face a commensurate challenge when considering entry into China.

- *Look at India as a long-term commitment.* Like China and every other emerging economy, India often suffers from not just unpredictable and schizophrenic government policies but also the fact that it is a low-income country open to players from every other country, including the United States, Europe, Japan, and South Korea. Thus companies often face brutal competition and thin margins. Yet if they are to have any hope of emerging as successful players over the next five to ten years, they must make investments now. Companies that cannot make a long-term commitment to India will find themselves giving up too early, before they have had the time to learn how to surmount the challenges that India presents and to capture the opportunities.

- *See India as part of the company's global strategy.* Chinese companies that look at their operations through a lens of "in India for the world" rather than "in India for India" are likely to realize much greater value from their investments and are also likely to be seen as friendly to the country by various arms of the government. Consider Lenovo. The company uses Bangalore as its global marketing hub with responsibility for various activities across fifty countries. Also, Lenovo is acutely aware that, in the PC business, global scale matters. Thus the company concluded, right from the beginning, that it could not hope to emerge as the global leader in PCs or smartphones without a leadership position in India. Similarly, look at Huawei. This company established a global R&D center in Bangalore several years before it started marketing and sales activities in the country. The R&D center employs more than two thousand engineers and is Huawei's largest R&D center outside China. It is not only a key pillar of Huawei's global technical strength but also has played an important role in easing the Indian government's ongoing security concerns about the company's equipment in the country's telecom network.

● *Be very cautious and selective when entering into a joint venture.* As we have seen in the cases in this chapter, TBEA, Huawei, Lenovo, and Haier operate wholly owned subsidiaries in India. In contrast, TWBB and Xinxing Heavy Machinery operate via joint ventures. We also saw that Haier's initial JV in 1999 proved to be a dud and slowed the company down by at least a couple of years. Except in those cases in which government policy dictates that the foreign company must form a joint venture (as in the case of multibrand retailing in India), companies need to carefully evaluate the need for a joint venture as well as the benefits, costs, and risks that may accompany setting up a joint venture with a particular partner. Setting up a JV with the wrong partner is almost as bad as marrying the wrong individual in one's personal life. It can be very costly in terms of time, money, and headaches. Equally important, exit from the JV may be difficult and quite costly.

It's important to guard against the risk of strategic conflict and mistrust. It's also important to agree on exit mechanisms and breakup terms in advance.

- *Engage with India as a country.* Every company knows that the direct stakeholders (customers, employees, suppliers, and banks) are important. However, many companies forget that the media and the government can be equally important stakeholders—perhaps even more important. This is especially true for Chinese companies in India, which operate in an environment of mistrust at national levels. Also, Chinese companies suffer, often unduly, from the perception that they bring shoddy, low-quality products to India. Given these realities, it is important for a Chinese company to develop a strategy that will help in persuading all key stakeholders that the company's operations in India present a win-win rather than a win-lose outcome. It is also important to remember that, even more so than in China, local governments in India may have policies and agendas that differ sharply from those of the central government. In China, the common saying is "Mountains are high and the emperor is far away." This saying applies even more forcefully in India, as many local officials there operate with the belief that the emperor is asleep and may not wake up for quite some time.

- *Beware of tough competition, and don't become complacent.* Besides the Europeans and the Americans, the Japanese and the South Koreans are also all over India. Many have operated in India much longer than the Chinese entrants. Lenovo competes with HP, Dell, Samsung, and LG. Huawei competes with Ericsson, Nokia, Alcatel-Lucent, and Cisco.

Haier competes with LG, Samsung, and Whirlpool. Shanghai Electric competes with ABB, Siemens, GE, and Toshiba. Almost every industry faces brutal competition. As the Indian market becomes larger and more open, the stakes will only become greater. Any Chinese company that takes its eyes off the ball and becomes complacent is likely to find itself crushed by more committed and more nimble competitors.

- *Above all, be a rapid learner.* It is a truism that whenever any company enters a new market, at least some of its assumptions will prove to be absurdly wrong. This is even more true when the two countries are as starkly different in some important respects as China and India. Further, internally, India is far more diverse than China in a host of dimensions—income levels, language, religion, climate, and political leanings. Thus, knowing New Delhi, Bangalore, or Mumbai well says little about whether you know India well. And like China, India is changing rapidly. Thus it's critical to make sure that one is not trapped in the mindset of 2010 when planning for 2020.

8

A China Roadmap for Indian Companies

November 2020—The conference room of the Confederation of Indian Industry (CII) in New Delhi was being readied for a major event: a grand signing ceremony of two major deals that were to be announced that afternoon. The director general of CII was smiling quietly despite the stress of the last-minute arrangements. A consortium of companies from China's rail sector would be signing a joint venture agreement with Indian Railways for the manufacture and installation of high-speed locomotives and rolling stock that would transform the speeds of major express trains by a factor of three. The journey between Mumbai and Delhi would be reduced to less than four hours—similar to that between Shanghai and Beijing. The China Development Bank had agreed to fund this RMB 30 billion project with a ten-year soft loan. Meanwhile, in the other conference room, one of India's top pharma companies would be signing a major licensing deal with the Chinese Academy of Sciences (CAS) to introduce an oncology drug developed in India for the Chinese health care market. The licensing deal would be worth several billion yuan over ten years. Under a parallel agreement, CAS would be setting up a joint R&D lab in Hangzhou, linked to the company's labs in India. Biotech scientists from both countries would work collaboratively on future drug development. The cost of such an R&D program would be half of what it would be in the United States, and the resulting products would be available to consumers worldwide.

Welcome to a possible new world in 2020, when India and China may be cooperating closely to create synergies across a number of business sectors. Since World War II, the world has seen many historical enemies write a new chapter in their relationship and focus instead on mutual cooperation via investments and trade. Some, such as the EU, have built fairly tight arrangements covering both commerce and security. Others, such as Mercosur in Latin America and ASEAN in Southeast Asia, have focused largely on regional economic integration through trade and investment. We deem it a near certainty that by 2020 the economic relationship between India and China will be much broader and deeper than it is at present. The two sides may even be closer to resolving their border disagreements than they are today. Should this come about, economic linkages between the two nations would grow even more rapidly.

We also believe that manufacturing, rather than agriculture or services, is likely to emerge as the primary driver of growth in economic ties between the two Asian neighbors. For a long time, Indian planners have been attempting to increase the contribution of manufacturing to the country's GDP. According to the twelfth Five-Year Plan, the current goal is to expand the contribution of manufacturing from the current level of about 16 percent to 25 percent or greater by 2025. To date, part of the challenge has been the fact that the focus has remained largely on addressing domestic needs rather than also developing a plan for export-oriented manufacturing. Other well-known hurdles include problems with land acquisition, onerous labor laws, lack of adequate skills, and poor infrastructure, all of which result in a woefully inadequate logistics chain. If India is to grow its economy at a sustained pace of 7 to 8 percent or faster, it will have to become a force in manufacturing—for both domestic markets as well as exports. Leadership in services, though exemplary, will not be enough to create much-needed jobs, compete in export markets, and leverage India's creative capabilities and high-end engineering skills. India needs to embrace the supply chain and logistics infrastructure that stretches across Asia into North America and Europe.

Given the well-known challenges of rising wage costs, shortage of blue-collar workers, and substantial pressure to go green, China will continue to upscale its manufacturing sector to create a much more sophisticated manufacturing base. In this endeavor, China will continue to avail itself of several inherent advantages:

- A population of over a billion consumers, which gives its companies a large domestic market and consequently scale

- Use of trained workers and a substantial increase in automation and process improvements, which will keep improving productivity
- A well-developed logistics supply chain, which includes a large pool of component vendors and is globally connected via transportation hubs and logistics depots

It is clear that a central pillar of China's new manufacturing roadmap will be a focus on higher value-added products. China will also give priority to the services sector, which is not only environmentally friendly but can absorb the growing number of white collar and knowledge workers. These priorities will go hand-in-hand with upskilling the work force and placing a much greater emphasis on innovation. At the same time, the country will attempt to mitigate the upward pressure on wages by offering major concessions to the industry to relocate to the less-developed western regions. Currently, just three major urban clusters—the Pearl River Delta centered around Guangdong province, the Yangtze river delta centered around Shanghai, and the Bejing-Tianjin region in the north—produce nearly half of China's GDP. This will change with other regions slowly taking over, as businesses continue their inland migration. Firms operating in or entering the Chinese market in this decade will have to keep this in mind, and their strategies will need to take into account the changing manufacturing landscape of China.

If India wants to benefit from this restructuring in China and ramp up its own manufacturing, its firms will have to focus increasingly on manufacturing-for-exports. They will need to become suppliers to China-based original equipment manufacturers (OEMs) by setting up a network of factories in both India and China. In addition, India will have to encourage Chinese manufacturers to locate some of their production in India by making their entry easier in special manufacturing zones that enable hassle-free entry. As Chinese firms grow in India and see the country's manufacturing strengths at close quarters, they will be better prepared to outsource some of their own production to Indian firms that are operating in both India and China. We are already beginning to witness this in the case of auto components, where major automotive OEMs have set up large assembly operations in China. They now expect Indian auto component firms to set up manufacturing and subassembly shops in China also and to become part of their global ecosystem. This interlinking could also be a cure for the long-term trade deficit that India runs with China—in a way that is beneficial to both countries while allowing Indian firms to understand the Chinese ecosystem before embarking on major investments in China.

Sundaram Fasteners Limited ("Sundaram"), a unit of India's US$6 billion revenue TVS Group, illustrates these dynamics well. In 2012, we interviewed Prem Kumar, then president of Sundaram China. With 2012 revenues of about US$400 million, Sundaram manufactures a variety of automotive components. The company is renowned for the quality of its products. It was the first Indian company to receive ISO 9000 certification and the only Indian company to receive a Best Supplier Award from General Motors. To meet the increasing requirements of its global customers, Sundaram has systematically expanded its network of manufacturing facilities. Following acquisitions in the United Kingdom and Germany, it set up a manufacturing facility in China in 2004. After an initial period of exports back to India, by 2006 Sundaram China had begun also exporting to global customers in Western markets and looking for opportunities to serve customers within China. The latter strategy became crucial after the global financial crisis of 2008–09 when the Western markets dried up. By 2012, Sundaram China was selling mostly to the Chinese subsidiaries of global customers such as Cummins and Caterpillar. Building on this history, the company's leaders were optimistic about signing up domestic Chinese companies also as their customers. Within China, Sundaram had beaten Chinese competitors in becoming a preferred supplier to prestigious Western multinationals. This success also held the promise of giving the company a high degree of credibility with Chinese customers.

In the rest of this chapter, we advance a set of *strategic guidelines* that Indian companies can use to design their moves in China.

THINK GLOBAL, NOT JUST IN-CHINA-FOR-CHINA

The starting point in developing a strategy for China is to place China in the context of the company's global (or, in some cases, regional) strategy. A global perspective can significantly increase the likelihood of success in China. It can also help the company become stronger globally.

Given the importance of local knowledge and relationships and the brutality of competition within China, it is hard to imagine how any foreign company can succeed in China by adopting a largely in-China-for-China perspective. The new entrant will start with no competitive advantage over entrenched incumbents and is likely to lose out rather quickly. The prospects for success in China improve dramatically when the new entrant leverages the firm's existing assets, relationships, and capabilities in shaping the initial foray into China. The preexisting strengths from outside China enable the company to achieve traction and start building local strengths to penetrate the Chinese market more deeply. For example, many Singaporean companies have entered China by leveraging their capabilities in urban planning and project management (where Singapore is one of the world's leaders) before branching into other segments of the domestic market within China. Tata Consultancy Services leveraged its relationship with GE, its largest global customer, to enter China by setting up a delivery center in Hangzhou for exporting software to captive global clients before branching out into the domestic Chinese market. Mahindra and NIIT chose to leverage their inherent strengths in tractor manufacturing and IT education, respectively (where they had built world class competencies), to enter the domestic Chinese market.

Adopting a global lens for designing an entry strategy for China can also motivate the company's leaders to explore not just a direct but also an indirect route into China. As the highly successful case of Tata Motors in China (discussed in Chapter Six)

229

illustrates, an indirect route via a third country can open up opportunities to succeed in China in contexts where a direct route may appear to have almost no prospects for success. India currently does not enjoy a strong global brand image in cars the way it does in sectors such as IT and generic pharmaceuticals. Also, even in India, Tata Motors is a smaller player in passenger cars. Thus, pursuing a direct route into China would have been extremely risky. However, the company has succeeded in China's luxury auto market by pursuing an indirect route; that is, leveraging the technological and brand strengths of Jaguar Land Rover, its U.K.-based subsidiary.

Another major benefit of adopting a global perspective when designing a strategy for China is that such a perspective can significantly expand the value that a foreign entrant could potentially derive from entry into China. Possible opportunities for such value expansion include capturing economies of global scale, strengthening relationships with global customers in B2B sectors, and diffusing China-focused innovations to other subsidiaries within the company's global network. Given its economic size, in most industries China is already the largest or one of the largest markets in the world. Thus success in China can enable the company to enjoy economies of global scale in areas such as R&D and procurement of raw materials and components. As we saw in Chapter Four, Mahindra Group is now pursuing such economies of global scale in the area of R&D for a new line of tractor engines that will be manufactured in both India and China. Additionally, as illustrated by the case of TCS and its relationships with GE and other global clients, being in China can not only strengthen the Indian company's relationships with global customers but also erect entry barriers for Chinese competitors. If an Indian company lacks a presence in China, the risk is great that Chinese competitors may start building relationships with the Indian company's global customers in China as the first step in winning their custom globally. The auto component sector also illustrates the opportunity for such economies of global scope. Global car companies are beginning to require their India-based auto component suppliers to set up operations in China. This is one of the reasons why Sundaram Fasteners went to China. It saw an opportunity to provide components to customers such as General Motors and Caterpillar, which valued the company's strengths in total quality management and wanted to buy from it not just in India but also in China.

Finally, adopting a global perspective for the company's China operations can accelerate the pace of innovation within the company on a worldwide basis. Being present in China will almost always force the company to innovate within the country as part and parcel of adapting to local imperatives. At least some of these innovations are likely to be globally relevant. This type of benefit is illustrated well by the case of NIIT in China, discussed in Chapter Five. NIIT invented the "NIIT Inside" model in China and has now taken this approach to other markets, including India.

RISK-PROOFING YOUR CHINA STRATEGY

As part of avoiding elementary mistakes (and getting trapped in self-fulfilling prophecies), it is important to invest in learning

231

about China before diving in. This can be done in one or more of several ways:

- Attending seminars in places such as Hong Kong and Singapore, the two most concentrated hubs for the Asian headquarters of the world's multinationals as well as professional advisory firms in accounting, investment banking, legal services, and management consulting
- Partnering with Chinese firms in India to understand the mindset and decision-making styles of Chinese executives
- Joining the India Business Forum in Beijing—set up by CII—which brings together executives from the larger Indian companies operating in China and is designed to be a forum for current and new members to learn from each other's experience

It can be extremely helpful if a senior member of the company's leadership team is an experienced China hand, well versed in the nuances of China. As an example, look at Anjanikumar Choudhari, who joined Mahindra Group as president of the Farm Equipment Sector in 1999. Just before joining the Mahindra Group, Choudhari had been based in China for five years, where he served as sales director for Unilever China and as vice chairman and managing director of Unilever Shanghai Sales Co.

Tata Group has built a core China group as a way to help its various companies learn about and move into China more quickly and with fewer mistakes. The Group has created a senior oversight team in Beijing as the umbrella that serves multiple roles—coordinating activities of the Tata companies already in China, assisting new subsidiaries in entering China, building an institutional brand with the government and potential partners, assisting in sourcing, and cultivating visibility on college campuses by recruiting graduates from top Chinese universities and rotating them for a year in various Tata entities worldwide. The umbrella office in Beijing also coordinates the activities of various Tata companies in the area of corporate social responsibility. Each year, the office also brings together the CEOs of all of the Group's China-based subsidiaries along with the senior-most executives from Group Headquarters in India. These mechanisms have created an unparalleled knowledge base and connections for the Tata Group in China resulting in revenues of about US$9 billion—that is, nearly 10 percent of the global turnover.

One can also reduce the risks of failure in China by first targeting a beachhead segment. One should think of the potential market in China not as a giant monolithic basket but as a potpourri of dozens of different segments (price points, demographics, geographic regions, Tier 1 versus Tier 2 versus Tier 3 cities, and so forth). Identify a beachhead segment and start from there. Mahindra started in China with small tractors. TCS started by first serving its global customers. JLR started by importing cars and SUVs from the United Kingdom. Similarly, Singaporean companies often start in China by focusing on market opportunities in urban infrastructure, an approach at which they excel.

An ideal beachhead segment is not necessarily a large one; rather, it is one with low barriers to entry and high chances of success. Starting with such a beachhead allows the company to get traction without a major downside. You also start building a local management pool and have a platform to start learning before figuring out how to move into adjacent segments. Companies that are diversified into multiple businesses, as is the case with most large Indian business groups, also need to decide which of these businesses should serve as the point of entry into China. Here also, the priority should be given to the business where the barriers to entry are the lowest and the chances of success highest. By way of example, Mahindra Group chose wisely when it decided to enter China first in the farm machinery rather than the automotive sector. At the time of Mahindra's entry into China, the tractor market was far more fragmented than the automotive market. This made entry easier and less risky.

DECIDING WHETHER TO PARTNER OR NOT

If regulations require partnering, then one does not have a choice. However, in some contexts in which regulations are not a factor, business logic may still suggest that partnering is better than going it alone. The key is to find good answers to several key questions:

- Do you need a partner or should you go it alone?
- If partnering, should it be a joint venture or a nonequity alliance?
- If a joint venture, what should be the ownership structure?
- What kind of a company would make a good partner?

- How should you manage the relationship with your JV partner?

Assuming that regulations are not a factor, whether or not you should partner depends very much on the strength of your existing capabilities and relationships in ensuring success in the targeted segments. For instance, had TCS chosen to focus only on its global customers, it might not have needed to set up a joint venture in China. On the other hand, such an approach would have made it much more difficult to penetrate the Chinese market for core banking software. Because all of the major banks are state-owned, having an arm of the Chinese government as a JV partner paid handsome dividends in terms of institutional legitimacy and credibility. In contrast, Jaguar Land Rover did not need to follow the joint venture route until such time as it decided to manufacture cars within China. Given the prestige of the JLR brands, selling imported cars needed a strong and extensive distribution and dealership network. Such a network could be built without getting into a joint venture relationship. However, now that JLR has decided to manufacture cars within China, it is bound by government policy to set up a 50-50 JV.

Assuming that government regulations are not a factor, acquiring a global or regional player with subsidiaries in China can be an effective route to enter China without needing a JV partner. WIPRO Consumer Products has done this successfully via acquisitions in Singapore and Malaysia and now has two Chinese subsidiaries with established local brands. These acquisitions provide WIPRO with an excellent base on which to build a bigger business in China.

Assuming that you choose to or have to set up a joint venture, it is important to be careful about who you chose as your partner and what the ownership structure should be. An ideal partner is one with which there is a high degree of complementarity but low risk of strategic and cultural conflict. Again, TCS serves as a good example. The Chinese government entities that partnered with TCS brought legitimacy but had no expertise in software and IT services, exactly the mirror image of what TCS brought to the JV. Also, these entities had no commercial goal of "learning" from TCS in the hope of one day becoming a competitor to TCS. In short, there was high complementarity but low risk of strategic conflict.

In B2B sectors, it is not uncommon for your potential JV partner to be a provincial- or city-owned state-owned enterprise (SOE), which historically owned the plant or distribution in a particular area. As in the cases of TCS and Mahindra, SOE partners can prove to be very helpful, especially if they have a minority stake and thus largely a supportive role. However, it is important to remember that, even if they have a minority stake, SOE partners can be a double-edged sword. It is extremely critical to maintain a good relationship right up to the top leadership level. Also note that, often enough, the priority of an SOE may be to build capacity and increase employment while margins, productivity, and the bottom line are all secondary. Thus it's important to think through how you will align your own company's goals with the SOE partner's.

If a company is considering partnering with a private sector party rather than state-owned entity in China, it is often critical to hire experienced advisors, including forensic advisors, to undertake thorough due diligence. Does the potential partner really own the assets (for example, land and buildings) that it claims to own? Who owns the brands—the company or certain individuals? Are the accounting statements legitimate or just one of a multiple set of books that the company's founder maintains? These are just some of the questions to which one would need clear and valid answers. Otherwise, the journey into China can become needlessly perilous.

Given the high growth rates in China, the aspiration levels of JV partners are often high. Thus the valuations can be demanding, especially if it is a well-performing company. Trying to buy an underperforming company on the cheap may not be very wise because the Indian company's lack of knowledge about the Chinese market and Chinese culture would prevent it from figuring out why the company is underperforming and then taking the needed corrective actions. If possible, it is advisable to aim for majority control, preferably with a 70-percent or larger equity stake, as Chinese law gives the majority shareholder considerable leeway in running the firm, similar to the Indian case of 76-percent shareholding. Even if you start with an initial stake of 51 percent, it may be possible to agree on a path toward a 70-percent or greater ownership stake. As with all JVs, the companies should agree on exit terms in advance. If at all possible, it's also important to agree in advance that any conflicts would be resolved via arbitration outside China rather than in Chinese courts.

In terms of managing the relationship with a JV partner, it is hard to overstate the importance of transparent and frequent communications. The directors and senior managers of

Chinese firms usually do not know or understand India well. Thus arranging periodic field trips to the Indian company's factories and offices in India and elsewhere can be very useful in instilling confidence that the Indian company is a long-term and capable player that can help grow the business in China. Such visits also help the partners to develop and sustain a common vision and reduce the likelihood of misunderstanding.

Once the JV agreement is in place, it is useful to have a local person serve as the chairman—ideally a well-connected professional or former bureaucrat who will be neutral and give the JV enhanced status with government bodies. In Chinese law, the chairman is also the legal representative of the firm and theoretically can commit the firm with his or her own chop. Thus it is important to build legal safeguards around this risk. Although board composition often follows directly from the ownership structure, it is important to keep your partner fully informed in advance of any major plans, even if the partner has a minority stake. Ongoing and transparent dialogue between senior managers and local board members can be especially useful during a downturn. As is the case elsewhere in the world, in China the majority partner has the right to appoint the CEO, but it is considered good practice to seek approval from the local partner. If the CEO is an expat on assignment from India or a third country, one should appoint a local manager as the deputy CEO who will be trained to take on the CEO role at some point. This "two in a box" approach for senior management positions is very useful for succession planning in key roles. Firms that are not good at succession planning find it difficult to retain local talent, as they can sense the presence of a glass ceiling.

MANAGING RELATIONSHIPS WITH THE GOVERNMENT

Like Brahma, Vishnu, and Mahesh, the state is omnipresent in China and thus always a "silent partner." Any firm operating in China must necessarily understand the nuances of dealing with the state and its subsidiaries at the central, provincial, city, and village levels. The best business plans will fail if relevant officials turn against them, and state decisions can profoundly affect the business opportunities available to any firm. Government functionaries, especially at the local level (such as mayors and vice-mayors), tend to be very pro-business and actively seek investments and assist new businesses in setting up and scaling up. It is important to note, however, that China is changing rapidly. This is equally true of government policies and priorities. Thus, although it is critical to understand the priorities laid out in the most recent five year plan, it is equally critical to stay updated on any changes and new developments.

As we noted earlier in Chapter Two, in the Chinese political system, there is no separation of powers between the state (that is, the government) and the Communist Party. The Party is the dominant power. Foreign executives must remember that, even though they may be dealing with government officials, key decisions are likely to be finalized only after consultation with Party representatives. Bear in mind also that, within the overall framework of a command-and-control system, it would be wrong to think of the Chinese government as monolithic—especially today. Decision-making power is widely dispersed across various ministries as well as between the center and various provincial and local governments, who enjoy considerable autonomy. Thus getting approvals at one level is no guarantee that you will not run into roadblocks at another level. Increasingly, one also finds open disagreement between various arms of the government on contentious issues that require trade-offs, such as removing controls on the currency versus promoting exports, pursuing economic growth versus protecting the environment, and so forth. Given these disagreements, it is becoming increasingly important for business leaders to try and understand the dynamics of political power within China in order to be smarter at anticipating future policies or the speed with which existing policies may come to be implemented.

BUILDING PRODUCT AND INSTITUTIONAL BRANDS

For any new entrant wishing to expand in China, brand recognition is a major challenge. China is a rapidly growing market with myriads of local and global brands. Also, unlike India, English is neither the official nor a commonly spoken language. Thus for a new entrant from India, building a brand from scratch can not only be very costly but also take a long time. If possible, a much faster approach is to acquire an existing local or "Western" brand with some degree of cachet. Tata Motors' success in China owes much to the fact that it operates there through British brands Jaguar and Land Rover. Similarly, Mahindra Tractors has chosen to operate in China by using the local brand names acquired through its joint ventures. Mahindra Group is now looking at entering the Chinese market for SUVs via its South Korean subsidiary SsangYong.

WIPRO has also entered the Chinese market for consumer goods by acquiring Singaporean and Malaysian companies that already have brands in China.

Brand building in China requires a company to position itself not only among the target customers but also among two other key constituencies—the government and potential new hires. These constituencies are important as being both socially conscious and committed to China. Chinese employees, media, and government bodies will generally embrace companies that are seen as committed to growth, to development of talent, and to protecting the environment. In this regard, operating in China is not all that different from operating in India.

Many new entrants to China wrongly assume that, because the media is tightly controlled by the state, using public relations firms and advertising agencies will yield limited value. Although it is indeed true that government control is exceptionally strong in the case of political news, companies are generally quite free to disseminate business-related news. People follow business and economics news widely and with great enthusiasm, and the media are saturated with commercials.

MANAGING TALENT

In 2013, China produced seven million college graduates, up from one million in 2001. Thus when it comes to finding talent, the challenge is one not of raw numbers, but of attracting and keeping the best talent and ensuring that people remain engaged and productive.

Given the rapid growth of the Chinese economy, people have come to expect frequent promotions (often in as short a time as twelve to eighteen months) and salary adjustments. As a correlate, turnover rates, especially among professional staff, can be as high as 20 to 40 percent per year. It is important, therefore, for managers to make sure not only that compensation is on a par with the market but also that other nonmonetary ties will keep top talent with the company. One effective mechanism to achieve multiple goals—developing employees' skills, cultivating loyalty, and also reducing turnover—is deferred compensation tied to investment in training and development. Depending on the specifics of the situation, deferred compensation can be designed in one or more of several ways: stock options or phantom shares that vest over time, subsidized loans for the purchase of a car or an apartment, and retention bonds. As an example of how retention bonds can be designed, consider the case of a Western industrial products company with a sizeable presence in China. As the Shanghai-based director of HR explained to us:

> We carry out a fair bit of management training. The programs can last anywhere from three to four weeks, to even six months in some cases. For a three- to four-week program, taking into account the direct costs of training, hotel and travel expenses, and lost salary, it may cost us $20,000. I have a policy that, if we send somebody for training abroad, the person must sign a two-year bond. If they leave before the two-year period, they must pay the company back what it cost us to send them for training. Also, if somebody does not want to sign a bond, then we will not invest in training them. In addition to this training-related bond, we have also signed

two-year or three-year retention bonds with several of our key managers. If they stay through the bond period, they get a sizeable bonus, which can be as high as 50 percent of annual salary.

Emotional and intellectual bonds are noneconomic ties that bind an employee to the organization. Emotional ties are a function of whether the employee views the company as a caring organization that is sensitive and responsive to the broader needs not just of the employee but also of the society to which the employee belongs. Factors that can nurture emotional bonds include the following:

- Is your company a fun place to work or not?
- Is your company sensitive to local holidays and festivals?
- Does your company build a sense of community within its local organization or do employees remain purely as individuals with no emotional ties to each other?
- Does your company go above and beyond its contractual responsibilities in times of personal emergency and distress for an employee?
- Does your company's agenda within China include making a contribution to the country's social needs or is the agenda solely economic?
- Does your company see China as its permanent home or is it acting merely as a "foreign tourist" or "foreign trader"?
- In times of national emergency (such as an earthquake or a typhoon), does your company respond with proactive and genuine care or is its response viewed as largely perfunctory?

Intellectual bonds are a function of whether or not the employee understands, agrees with, and likes the company's strategic direction and the opportunities that it provides for professional development. Factors that drive intellectual bonding include the following:

- Does your company share its vision and strategy with the employees, or do they operate largely in the dark with no sense for the bigger picture?
- Do your employees in China agree with and like the company's vision and strategy?
- Do the employees view your company as an organization that will help them acquire important skills and capabilities, or do they view their current tasks as just a job to earn a living?
- Are the employees proud of the fact that they work for your company?

These are illustrative rather than comprehensive lists of the factors that are likely to matter in cultivating emotional and intellectual bonds. Such bonds will not reduce the necessity of keeping your compensation structure competitive with market conditions. However, they will almost certainly have a notable impact on how productive the employees are, how effective they are in drawing new talent to the company, and your company's attrition rate in China. The economic impact of advantages in these areas could well swamp any disadvantages from rising compensation levels.

Even though most of your employees in China are likely to be local nationals, it is almost always necessary to have a small number of expatriate managers and technical staff in key positions. Of course, sending expatriates to China is expensive. However, they can play a very critical role in several areas, such as

- Transferring corporate systems, processes, and codes of conduct to the Chinese subsidiary
- Diffusing technical knowledge to and/or from the Chinese operations and ensuring managerial and financial control over the local operations
- Facilitating integration between the Chinese operations and those in India or elsewhere
- Keeping colleagues and corporate leaders in India informed about developments in China

Our experience and research suggest that Indian expatriates generally find it easy to adjust to the Chinese environment because the societies share a common Asian cultural background. Relations between Chinese and Indian staff tend to be friendly and easygoing. Younger Chinese are generally eager to learn more about India and are interested in Bollywood and other aspects of Indian culture.

TREATING YOUR CHINA JOURNEY AS A LEARNING PROCESS

China is a complex and rapidly changing society and, in many ways, quite different from India. No matter how well you prepare yourself in advance, you will find that at least some of your assumptions are simply wrong. This is no different from the experience of any firm that has ever crossed international borders, including U.S.-based firms when they have entered contiguous and relatively familiar markets such as Canada and Mexico. The certainty that your assumptions are at least partially wrong does not in the least imply that you should not prepare well in advance. It just means that, aside from advance preparation, it is equally important to keep an open mind and to be prepared to learn rapidly.

There are at least four reasons why being a good learner is critical to succeeding in China. First, despite important similarities (population size, Asian heritage, developing country status), China is also very different from India in several important respects (language, per capita incomes, materialism, pragmatism, belief in hard rather than soft power, and so on). Thus, when Indians look at China through their naturally Indian lenses, it is easy to fall prey to stereotyping rather than gaining true understanding. Second, China is an ancient and complex society. Contemporary China is a hybrid of several competing ideologies—Taoism, Confucianism, Buddhism, communism, and capitalism. As in the proverbial story of the blind men and the elephant, it is easy to assume that you understand China when all you understand is just one tiny aspect of it. Third, China is internally very diverse, the most obvious diversity being among income levels. The populations of the ten richest cities in China (including Beijing, Shanghai, and Shenzhen) put together make up less than 10 percent of China's population. Thus knowing Beijing and Shanghai well can easily lull an outsider into falsely assuming that they know China well. Last but not least, China is changing rapidly—not just economically but also socially and even politically. Thus even if you were an expert on China in 2010, it's quite likely that, in many important ways, your knowledge of China may be obsolete by 2015.

The sole agenda of some of the early travelers from India to China (such as Kumarajiva) and China to India (Fa Xian) was purely to learn from each other. We do not mean to suggest that today's business leaders should abandon more "mundane" goals such as revenues, profits, and shareholder value. We do believe, however, that businessmen and women who cross the Himalayas with a learning mindset are more likely to end up not just wiser but also more successful. We encourage you to think of China not just as a playground but also as a school—one that can enrich your life as well as your business.

Notes

Chapter One

1. "India visit has helped expand strategic thrust: Li Keqiang," *LiveMint*, May 22, 2013.
2. In the October 2013 edition of the *World Economic Outlook*, the International Monetary Fund forecasts that the GDPs of China and India are likely to grow at 7.0 percent and 6.7 percent, respectively, during the five-year period 2013–2018.
3. Based on data from the United Nations Conference on Trade and Development (www.unctad.org).
4. Based on interviews with officers at the Chinese and Indian embassies in New Delhi and Beijing, respectively.
5. "Chinese film *Gold Struck* to go on floor soon," *Bollywood Hungama*, August 16, 2013 (www.bollywoodhungama.com); "Indo-Chinese film *Gold Struck* to go on floors this December," *Business Standard*, August 18, 2013; "China gives greenlight to first 'Made in China' Bollywood film," *Hindu*, December 29, 2010.
6. For a recent example of China's ongoing support for Pakistan, see Saeed Shah, "China-Pakistan reactor deal spurs concern," *Wall Street Journal*, October 16, 2013, p. A11. According to this report, China has agreed to supply two large nuclear power reactors worth about US$ 9.1 billion to its long-time ally. It will also finance 80 percent of the cost on very generous terms. The author of the article notes, "For Islamabad, the pact with China counters a nuclear-energy accord signed with the U.S. under then-president George W. Bush. Pakistan regards that arrangement as giving India an unfair potential strategic advantage in nuclear weapons."
7. Indian leaders often use the terms "religious leader" and "honored guest" when describing the Dalai Lama's stay in India.
8. "Indian foreign policy in the 21st century: Challenges and opportunities," address by Ambassador Nirupama Rao at the Hudson Institute, March 22, 2012.

9. Xinhua news agency report, as quoted in Ananth Krishnan, "India, China should deepen military ties: Xi Jinping," *Hindu*, March 28, 2013.

10. "Premier Li Keqiang's visit: India and China in border row pledge," *BBC News*, May 20, 2013.

11. Murray Scot Tanner with Kerry B. Dumbaugh and Ian M. Easton, "Distracted antagonists, wary partners: China and India assess their security relations," Center for Naval Analyses, September 2011.

12. "China unveils 5-point formula to improve ties with India," *Hindu*, March 19, 2013 (http://www.thehindubusinessline.com/news/international/china-unveils-5point-formula-to-improve-ties-with-india/article4524944.ece).

13. Based on data from UNCTAD (www.unctad.org).

14. Based on data from the United Nations Population Division.

15. *China 2030*, The World Bank, February 2012.

16. *World Economic Outlook*, International Monetary Fund, October 2013, p. 21.

17. *World Economic Outlook*, International Monetary Fund, October 2013.

18. See Bob Davis and Richard Silk, "China to test looser grip on economy: New free-trade zone in Shanghai opens," *Wall Street Journal*, September 27, 2013 (http://online.wsj.com/news/articles/SB100014240527023047958045791006402456 13408).

19. For more extended arguments on this point, see Anil K. Gupta and Haiyan Wang, "Let China supply India's public works boom," *Wall Street Journal*, October 22, 2012 (http://online.wsj.com/news/articles/SB100008723963904443584045776044 593624357120).

20. As an example, see "ADAG gets $3 billion loan from China banks, StanChart," *Reuters*, December 15, 2010 (http://www.reuters.com/article/2010/12/15/adag-chineseloan-idUSSGE6BE02N20101215). This news report stated: "India's Reliance Communications and Reliance Power, both part of the Anil Dhirubhai Ambani Group (ADAG), will borrow a total of $3 billion in long-term loans mostly from Chinese banks to be used in refinancing existing debt and for equipment purchases."

21. There are no reliable data on bilateral FDI investments. For India and China, estimates that we came across vary wildly. These figures are based on interviews with officers at the Chinese and Indian embassies in New Delhi and Beijing, respectively.

22. "Chinese explore setting up industrial parks in UP, Haryana," *Economic Times*, October 20, 2013.

Chapter Two

1. See *China 2030*. The World Bank, 2012; also Anil K. Gupta and Haiyan Wang, "Corporate strategies for a slowing China—Part 1" and "Corporate strategies for a slowing China—Part 2," *Bloomberg Businessweek*, September 24 & 26, 2012 (http://www.businessweek.com/articles/2012–09–24/corporate-strategies-for-a-slowing-china-part-1 and http://www.businessweek.com/articles/2012–09–26/corporate-strategies-for-a-slowing-china-part-2).

2. UNCTAD Statistics.

3. Data from United Nations World Population Division (http://esa.un.org/unpd/wpp/unpp/panel_indicators.htm).

4. Data from *World Development Indicators*, The World Bank (http://databank.world bank.org/data/views/variableSelection/selectvariables.aspx?source=world-development-indicators).

5. Data from www.tradingeconomics.com and National Bureau of Statistics of China.

6. "Foxconn to replace workers with 1 million robots in three years," *Xinhua News Agency*, July 23, 2011 (http://news.xinhuanet.com/english2010/china/2011–07/30/c_131018764.htm).

7. PM 2.5 refers to particulate matter 2.5 micrometers or smaller in diameter. Smaller particles in the air are particularly dangerous to the lungs as they can go deep inside the lungs and become carcinogens. A PM 2.5 reading of 15 means 15 micrograms of PM 2.5 per cubic meter of air.

8. "Air quality and health," World Health Organization, September 2011 (http://www.who.int/mediacentre/factsheets/fs313/en/).

9. "China to inspect air pollution control," *China Daily*, October 24, 2013 (http://usa.chinadaily.com.cn/business/2013–10/24/content_17056512.htm).

10. Amartya Sen, *The argumentative Indian* (New York: Picador, 2006).

11. See www.transparency.org.

12. "Gini out of the bottle," *Economist*, January 26, 2013 (http://www.economist.com/news/china/21570749-gini-out-bottle).

13. "China's Gini index at 0.61, University report says," *Caixin Online*, December 12, 2012 (http://english.caixin.com/2012–12–10/100470648.html).

14. See Anil K. Gupta and Haiyan Wang, "Beat the odds in cross-border joint ventures," *Harvard Business Review*, Blog Network, October 9, 2013 (http://blogs.hbr.org/anil-gupta-and-haiyan-wang/).

15. "Chinese authorities find 22 more fake stores," *Reuters*, August 11, 2011 (http://www.reuters.com/article/2011/08/11/us-apple-china-fake-idUSTRE77A3U820110811).

16. For more details, see also Anil K. Gupta and Haiyan Wang, "Safeguarding your intellectual property in China," *Bloomberg Businessweek*, May 20, 2011.

Chapter Three

1. "Li Keqiang visits TCS in India: Cyrus Pallonji Mistry, Chairman Tata Group, says China important for growth of Tata Group," *Economic Times*, May 27, 2013.

2. Partha Iyengar, India country manager for Gartner Research, quoted in Saritha Rai, "India's TCS becomes the world's second most valuable IT services firm," *Forbes India*, September 2013 (http://www.forbes.com/sites/saritharai/2013/09/13/indias-tcs-is-second-most-valuable-it-services-firm-globally/).

3. A foreign company was not permitted to set up a branch office at that time.

Chapter Four

1. "Mahindra to use weak dollar to buy US factories," *Economic Times*, December 4, 2007.

2. Throughout this chapter, we use the terms "Mahindra and Mahindra" and "Mahindra Group" interchangeably and synonymously. This is consistent with how these terms are used by the company itself.

3. "Mahindra & Mahindra aims to grab number 3 position in China, U.S. tractor markets," *Economic Times*, February 21, 2012 (http://articles.economictimes.india times.com/2012–02–21/news/31082905_1_tractor-markets-tractors-sales-china).

4. Video interview with Anand Mahindra (http://www.mahindra.com/Who-We-Are/Our-Brand).

5. Video interview with Bharat Doshi (http://www.mahindra.com/Who-We-Are/Overview).

6. "Mahindra & Mahindra Ltd.—Farm Equipment Sector: Acquisition of Jiangling Tractor Company," Case # 907M35, Richard Ivey School of Business.

7. Ibid.

8. Pete Engardio, Michael Arndt, and Geri Smith, "Emerging Giants," *BusinessWeek*, July 30, 2006 (http://www.businessweek.com/stories/2006–07–30/emerging-giants).

9. Garret W. Davis, Dee von Bailey, and Katherine M. Chudoba, "Defining and meeting the demand for agricultural machinery in China," *International Food and Agribusiness Management Review*, 3(3), 2010.

10. Matthew Shane & Fred Gale, China: A study of dynamic growth. U.S. Department of Agriculture, 2004.

11. Authors' interviews with Harish Chavan, March 2012. Unless otherwise indicated, all subsequent Chavan quotes are from these interviews.

12. "Mahindra & Mahindra Ltd.—Farm Equipment Sector: Acquisition of Jiangling Tractor Company."

13. Vipin V. Nair, "India's Mahindra plans to make China a hub for tractor exports," *Bloomberg*, August 2, 2009.

14. "Mahindra & Mahindra aims to grab No 3 position in China, U.S. tractor markets."

Chapter Five

1. "A class act: Leader of an Indian firm engaged in information technology education in China looks beyond classroom," *China Daily* (*Asia Weekly*), January 14–20, 2011 (http://www.niit.com/investorrelations/Investor%20Newsletter/Q4Mar2011/document/a_class_act;china%20daily-asia-weekly;january14–20,2011.pdf).

2. "NIIT honoured as the most Influential IT Training Brand in China," September 30, 2009 (http://www.niit.com/newsandevents/Lists/NIIT%20News/disform Customv3.aspx?List=a325a1cf-a064–4573-b17a-3ce893a0d178&ID=181#sthash.uw3pBJ1L.dpbs).

3. Li Jing, "China's Bangalore," *China Daily* (*Business Weekly*), March 31, 2008 (http://www.chinadaily.com.cn/bw/2008–03/31/content_6576683.htm).

4. "NIIT penetrates China with IT teaching in English," *Hindustan Times*, April 23, 2006 (http://www.highbeam.com/doc/1P3–1026271341.html).

Chapter Six

1. Lijee Philip, "China to be Tata Motors' biggest revenue driver this fiscal year," *Economic Times*, August 20, 2013 (http://articles.economictimes.indiatimes.com/2013 -08-20/news/41429076_1_tata-motors-jaguar-land-rover-mahantesh-sabarad).
2. Dan Neil, "Given room to grow, Range Rover blossoms," *Wall Street Journal*, November 23–24, 2013, p. D12.
3. Marietta Cauchi, "Tata pushes upscale SUVs," *Wall Street Journal*, February 12, 2013 (http://online.wsj.com/news/articles/SB10001424127887323511804578300101121190148).
4. Han Tianyang, "Jaguar Land Rover revving up for China," *China Daily*, April 15, 2011 (http://www.chinadaily.com.cn/cndy/2011–04/15/content_12330130.htm).
5. "Rising numbers, new products by Jaguar Land Rover," *China Daily*, November 26, 2012 (http://www.chinadaily.com.cn/business/2012–11/26/content_15961776 .htm).
6. Liang Fei, "Jaguar Land Rover, Chery moving ahead," *Global Times*, October 25, 2013 (http://www.globaltimes.cn/content/820230.shtml#.UqMwTfRDuSo).

Chapter Seven

1. "Friend, enemy, rival, investor: How can India make its economic relations with China less lopsided?" *Economist*, June 30, 2012 (http://www.economist.com/node /21557764).
2. See Ken Davies, *Outbound FDI from China and its policy context 2012*. Columbia FDI Profiles, Vale Columbia Center, Columbia University, June 7, 2012; Thilo Hanemann, *Chinese investment: Europe vs. the United States*. Rhodium Group, February 25, 2013; Thilo Hanemann & Daniel H. Rosen, *China's international investment position: An update*. Rhodium Group, April 23, 2013.
3. Shanghai Automotive Industries Corporation (SAIC) acquired a 50-percent stake in General Motors India in 2009. However, in 2012, SAIC and GM restructured the ownership of the Indian operations. SAIC's stake is now about 7 percent, with General Motors owning 93 percent. See Amit Raj, "GM buys 43% stake of SAIC in India operations," LiveMINT, October 16, 2012 (http://www.livemint.com /Companies/VZMqBsgHkM9DkPbDFe0gNJ/GM-buys-43-stake-of-SAIC-in-India-operations.html).
4. M. Ramesh, "14% import duty on power gear inadequate: BHEL chief," *Hindu Business Line*, August 11, 2012 (http://www.thehindubusinessline.com/companies /article3754250.ece).
5. Utpal Bhaskar, "TBEA, BHEL in talks for partnership," *liveMINT*, December 30, 2009 (http://www.livemint.com/Home-Page/LO9S4S4CZvMnCgBoGYRW2O /TBEA-Bhel-in-talks-for-partnership.html).
6. "Chinese group plans unit near Vadodara," *Business Standard*, May 27, 2011 (http://www.business-standard.com/article/companies/chinese-group-plans-unit-near-vadodara-111052700086_1.html).
7. "We see better and brighter future for T and D business," *Power Today*, June 2013 (http://www.powertoday.in/News.aspx?nId=ot55RHwa9UsZvhrtpqxmtg==).

8. Prashant Rupera, "Power dragons make Vadodara their battleground," *Times of India*, May 8, 2012 (http://articles.timesofindia.indiatimes.com/2012–05–08/vadodara/31626180_1_twbb-transformer-factory-ultra-high-voltage).

9. DI pipes are commonly used for the transmission and distribution of potable water. The iron used to manufacture such pipes is infused with spheroidal or nodular graphite. In order to inhibit corrosion, DI pipes also have inner linings (typically made from cement mortar) as well as external coatings (made from bonded zinc, asphalt, or water-based paint). Depending on the nature of the lining and encasing of the pipe, a DI pipe can have a lifespan of more than a hundred years.

10. World Steel Association, *World steel figures in 2013*.

11. "Speech of Ambassador Zhang Yan on the commissioning ceremony of Xindia Steel Limited," October 18, 2011. Embassy of the People's Republic of China in the Republic of India (http://in2.mofcom.gov.cn/article/biography/201110/20111007785294.shtml).

12. *Huawei: Cisco's Chinese challenger*. Case No. HKU599. Asia Case Research Centre, The University of Hong Kong, 2006.

13. "Huawei: The company that spooked the world," *Economist*, August 4, 2012 (http://www.economist.com/node/21559929).

14. Shilpa Phadnis, "Cisco stops hiring from Huawei in India," *Times of India*, July 17, 2013 (http://timesofindia.indiatimes.com/business/india-business/Cisco-stops-hiring-from-Huawei-in-India/articleshow/21113317.cms).

15. "Huawei: The company that spooked the world," *Economist*, August 4, 2012 (http://www.economist.com/node/21559929).

16. "Huawei to open global R&D centre in India," *Times of India*, June 25, 2012 (http://articles.timesofindia.indiatimes.com/2012–06–25/telecom/32408080_1_huawei-india-r-d-centre-research-and-development-centre).

17. Sunny Sen, "How ZTE, Huawei are hitting European rivals hard in India," *Business Today*, October 28, 2012 (http://businesstoday.intoday.in/story/huawei-zte-market-share-in-india/1/188935.html).

18. "Huawei to offer phantom shares to Indian employees," *Economic Times*, March 6, 2013 (http://articles.economictimes.indiatimes.com/2013–03–06/news/37500377_1_huawei-s-india-cai-liqun-china-s-huawei).

19. Ramprasad Lakshmimarayanan, V-P, Transactional Consumer Sales, Lenovo India. Quoted in "Lenovo: Replicating its success in India," *VARIndia*, January 2009 (http://varindia.webtenet.com/Jan_VarCorporate.htm).

20. Amar Babu, managing director, Lenovo India. Quoted in "Lenovo continues retail expansion in India, inaugurates its 400th LES Lite," *Financial Express*, July 31, 2011 (http://computer.financialexpress.com/20110731/expresschannelbusiness13.shtml).

21. "Lenovo emerges as top PC seller in India," *Economic Times*, May 15, 2013 (http://articles.economictimes.indiatimes.com/2012–05–15/news/31711729_1_indian-pc-market-lenovo-india-pc-penetration).

22. "Lenovo's protect and attack strategy helped it expand globally: Yang Yuanqing, Chairman and CEO, Lenovo Group," *Economic Times*, February 1, 2013 (http://articles.economictimes.indiatimes.com/2013–02–01/news/36684740_1_smartphones-lenovo-group-global-pc-market).

23. Sunny Sen, "Combining to conquer," *Business Today*, September 29, 2013 (http://businesstoday.intoday.in/story/hp-number-1-again-in-pcs-and-printers/1/1983 30.html).

24. Nikhil Celly, "Haier in India: Building presence in a mass market beyond China," Case #HKU978. Asia Case Research Centre, 2012.

25. "Haier, already a success, aims higher," *Knowledge@Wharton*, April 5, 2005 (http://knowledge.wharton.upenn.edu/article/haier-already-a-success-aims-higher/).

26. Tarun Khanna, Krishna Palepu, & Phillip Andrews, *Haier: Taking a Chinese Company global in 2011*, Harvard Business Review Case #9–712–408.

27. "Chinese company to enter white goods market," *Economic Times*, March 25, 2002 (http://articles.economictimes.indiatimes.com/2002–03–25/news/27336666_1_haier-indian-market-products).

28. "Haier sees growth at bottom of pyramid," *Economic Times*, July 3, 2006 (http://articles.economictimes.indiatimes.com/2006–07–03/news/27465466_1_mass-market-products-haier-india-high-end-products).

29. Mayura Shanbaug, "Haier's aggressive strategy," *Afternoon Dispatch & Courier*, January 17, 2011 (http://www.afternoondc.in/business-investment/haiers-aggressive-strategy/article_16479).

About the Authors

Anil K. Gupta is chairman, China India Institute, and the Michael D. Dingman Chair in Strategy, Globalization, and Entrepreneurship at the Smith School of Business, the University of Maryland at College Park. He is also a Visiting Professor at Tsinghua University, one of China's most elite universities, and has earlier served on the faculties of Stanford University, INSEAD, and Dartmouth College. He received a doctorate from the Harvard Business School, an MBA from the Indian Institute of Management at Ahmedabad, and a BTech from the Indian Institute of Technology at Kanpur.

Gupta is widely regarded as one of the world's leading experts on strategy, globalization, and emerging markets. He has been ranked by *Thinkers50* as one of the world's "most influential living management thinkers" and named by the *Economist* as one of the world's "superstars" in a cover story titled "Innovation in Emerging Economies." He is one of only three professors in the world to have been elected by his academic peers as a Lifetime Fellow of all three of the most prestigious bodies in the field: Academy of Management, Strategic Management Society, and Academy of International Business, with a combined membership of over twenty-five thousand scholars worldwide.

Gupta's other honors include receiving the Best Professor in Strategic Management Award from CMO Asia, recognition by *BusinessWeek* as an Outstanding Faculty in its *Guide to the Best B-Schools*, induction into the *Academy of Management Journals' Hall of Fame*, and listing by *Management International Review* as a "North American Superstar" for research in strategy and organization. He is also a regular participant at the World Economic Forum summits, including the annual meeting in Davos and the regional meetings in China, India, and the Middle East. He is also a member of the Forum's Global Agenda Council on Emerging Multinationals.

Gupta's earlier book, *Getting China and India Right* (Wiley, 2009), received the 2009 Axiom Book Awards' Silver Prize as one of the world's two best books on globalization/international business and was short-listed for the Asia Society's Annual Bernard Schwartz Book Award. He is also the author, coauthor, or coeditor of *Global Strategies for Emerging Asia* (Wiley, 2012), *The Quest for Global Dominance* (Wiley, 2008), *Smart Globalization* (Wiley, 2003), and *Global Strategy and Organization* (Wiley, 2003), as well as over seventy papers in leading academic journals.

Gupta serves as a columnist for *Bloomberg Businessweek*, as a contributing editor for *Chief Executive* magazine, and as a contributor to HBR.org. His opinion pieces have also been published in the *Wall Street Journal*, the *Financial Times*, *Chief*

Executive Magazine, Daily Telegraph, China Daily, the *Economic Times,* and other outlets. He has been interviewed by *Harvard Business Review, Economist,* the *Wall Street Journal,* the *Washington Post, USA Today, BusinessWeek, Forbes,* BBC, CNBC, Fox TV, Bloomberg TV, Reuters TV, New Delhi TV, and CCTV China, as well as other top-tier global media.

Gupta serves regularly as a keynote speaker at major conferences and corporate forums in the United States, Europe, Asia, Latin America, and Africa, including the World Economic Forum, *Economist* conferences, the *BusinessWeek* CEO Forum, *Chief Executive* magazine's CEO2CEO Summits, and the Yale CEO Summit. He has also served as a consultant, keynote speaker, and/or executive education faculty with some of the largest corporations in the world including GE, Chevron, Total, Wal-Mart, IBM, Coca-Cola, HSBC, Deutsche Bank, Rio Tinto, Indian Oil, Steel Authority of India, Huawei Technologies, and many others.

Gupta is an elected member of the board of directors of Origene Technologies (a U.S.- and China-based biotechnology company) and has previously served on the board of directors of several NYSE- and NASDAQ-listed companies. He also serves on the advisory boards of Asia Silicon Valley Connection and India Globalization Capital, and has previously served as an advisor to the U.S.-India Business Council.

Girija Pande is well known in Asia, having spent over three decades in the region working in senior capacities in a large multinational bank and a global information technology company. Currently, he heads Apex Avalon, a Singapore-based company that provides strategic consulting, research, and analysis to businesses in the Asia Pacific (APAC) market. His company is an equal JV between Apex Advisors of Singapore and Avalon Consulting, which has been ranked in the top ten strategy consulting organizations in the APAC region.

Pande spent the last eleven years with Tata Consultancy Services (TCS) as chairman/CEO of TCS APAC. TCS is one of Asia's largest technology companies, with a market capitalization of over US$55 billion. He was instrumental in setting up TCS's APAC headquarters in Singapore in 2001 and pioneered its business growth in the region. Under his leadership, the company expanded to over eleven thousand associates in fourteen countries. He was awarded the Best CEO Award by Singapore Government's HR Institute in 2010.

Pande was instrumental in developing the strategy for TCS's business in China and was also the vice chairman of TCS's JV with the Chinese Government. Today TCS has over two thousand associates in six Chinese cities. Pande's deep knowledge of Chinese industry and business practices led him to serve as an economic advisor to the mayor of Guangzhou, China's third-largest city. He is familiar with Mandarin and has developed high-level commercial contacts in China.

Pande has also served on many professional and government think tanks in Singapore and India. He was a member of the Manpower Council, set up by the Infocom Development Authority of the Government of Singapore, and serves on the Advisory Board of Singapore Management University. He also serves on the board of the Institute of South Asian Studies at the National University of Singapore, as well as on the board of the Singapore International Chamber of Commerce.

Pande serves on the board of Tata Communications International, one of the largest global players in the telecom market. He is also an independent director of Micro-Mechanics (a semiconductor tooling company) and Ascendas India REIT. He chaired the Singapore-based India Business Forum, affiliated with the Confederation of Indian Industry, for over five years. As part of his voluntary commitments to society, he also serves on the board of the National Council of Social Services, the Singapore Government's statutory board, which oversees all voluntary welfare organizations, and is a trustee of the Singapore Indian Development Association.

Pande holds an engineering degree and an MBA from the Indian Institute of Management at Ahmedabad. He was a banker with the ANZ Banking Group for over two decades and has extensive experience throughout Asia, with senior postings in South Korea, Hong Kong, Bahrain, and India. He was the executive chairman of ANZ Grindlays Asset Management Company in India and has served on the advisory boards of private equity funds focused on the Indian technology sector. He has also served on many high-level policy-planning committees of the Reserve Bank of India, as well as on the executive management committee of ASSOCHAM. He has been a speaker at the World Economic Forum in China and is often invited to speak on business and technology forums in Asia. He has also been interviewed by CNBC, Bloomberg TV, and other international media for his views on Asian and global business trends.

Pande is well known among business circles in Singapore, India, and China, and has wide-ranging contacts in all three countries.

Haiyan Wang is managing partner of China India Institute, a Washington, DC–based research consultancy with a focus on creating winning global strategies that leverage the transformational rise of China and India. She has also been an adjunct professor of strategy at INSEAD.

Wang has been listed by *Thinkers50* in "On the Guru Radar" and was short-listed for the 2011 Global Village Award. She has also been named as a "New Guru" by the *Economic Times*.

Wang co-writes a regular column for *Bloomberg Businessweek* and blogs for the *Harvard Business Review*. She is the coauthor of two highly acclaimed books, *Getting China and India Right*, which received the 2009 Axiom Book Awards' Silver Prize as one of the world's two best books on globalization and international business, and *The Quest for Global Dominance*.

Her opinion pieces have appeared in top international media such as the *Wall Street Journal*, *Businessweek*, the *Financial Times*, *Chief Executive*, *Wired*, the *Economic Times*, *China Daily*, the *Times of India*, and the *South China Morning Post*, as well as other outlets. She has also been frequently interviewed by CNBC, the *Wall Street Journal*, *Fox Business*, *India Today*, CNN *Expansión*, *Shanghai Daily*, *INSEAD Knowledge*, and other prominent business media.

A native of China, Wang has spent the last twenty years consulting for and managing multinational business operations in China and the United States in several different industry sectors. She speaks at major conferences such as the World Economic Forum's Summer Davos Summit, TEDx, *Economist*, CNN Expansión, and Brookings Institution talks, as well as corporate forums in the United States, Europe, Asia, and Latin America.

Wang was among the first batch of Chinese to study international business shortly after China embarked on economic reforms and opened its doors to the outside world. In the mid-1980s, she published several papers on China's foreign trade reform in Chinese journals such as *International Business* and *International Trade Tribune*.

In the United States, Wang began her career working as a management consultant with Princeton, NJ–based Kepner-Tregoe. She provided executive training and consulting services in the areas of strategic decision making, complex project management, and organizational process redesign. Her clients included some of the world's largest corporations: Johnson & Johnson, Corning, Sprint, and the Singapore-based Far East Ship Yard.

Wang also served as director of business development at E-Steel Corporation, a New York–based pioneer in e-marketplace in the global steel industry. At E-Steel, she led the company's efforts to form partnerships between the company and top Chinese steel producers such as BaoSteel. Wang has also served as a senior marketing and operations executive at PTI, Inc., a global manufacturer and wholesaler of consumer products with supply chain operations in the United States, China, and Vietnam. She helped to realign the company's strategic focus to service top retail chains such as Target, IKEA, Kohl's, and J.C. Penney.

Wang received a bachelor's degree in economics from Shanghai Institute of Foreign Trade and a master's degree in international business from the University of International Business and Economics in Beijing. She also holds an MBA from the University of Maryland at College Park.

Index